Mindful Willpower

Achieve Your Goals by Training Your Mind to Gain Focus, Build Better Habits, and Increase Self-Control

By: Devin White

ALL RIGHTS RESERVED

No part of this book may be reproduced, stored in a retrieval system, or transmitted in any form or by any means, electronic, mechanical, photocopying, recording, scanning, or otherwise, without the prior written permission of the publisher.

Limit of Liability/Disclaimer of Warranty: the publisher and the author make no representations or warranties with respect to the accuracy or completeness of the contents of this work and specifically disclaim all warranties, including without limitation warranties of fitness for a particular purpose. No warranty may be created or extended by sales or promotional materials. The advice and strategies contained herein may not be suitable for every situation. This work is sold with the understanding that the publisher is not engaged in rendering medical, legal or other professional advice or services. If professional assistance is required, the services of a competent professional person should be sought. Neither the publisher nor the author shall be liable for damages arising herefrom. The fact that an individual, organization or website is referred to in this work as a citation and/or potential source of further information does not mean that the author or the publisher endorses the information the individuals, organization or website may provide or recommendations they/it may make. Further, readers should be aware that websites listed on this work may have changed or disappeared between when this work was written and when it is read.

Table of Contents

Chapter 1: Mindfulness: Unlocking the Mystery 4

Chapter 2: Focus: Get Rid of Hocus Pocus 103

Chapter 3: The Goal Getter in You 113

Chapter 4: Self Control For the Soul 119

Chapter 5: Make Willpower Your Superpower 129

Chapter 6: Emotions! Regulate and Celebrate 133

Chapter 7: Happy Healthy Habits! 138

Chapter 8: Everyday Mindful Moments 141

References: 145

Chapter 1: Mindfulness: Unlocking the Mystery

"When we are mindful, deeply in touch with the present moment, our understanding of what is going on deepens, and we begin to be filled with acceptance, joy, peace, and love."
Thich Nhat Hanh

Mindfulness is a topic that has become popularized in today's mainstream society and you can thank Buddha for that! Now, it is your turn to take that leap into finding your own individual path towards mindfulness. If you are already familiar, take a stroll down memory lane, make some new connections, and be reminded of how this journey and practice of mindfulness can be rejuvenated as it is forever evolving through consistent growth and change.

The goal of mindfulness is to stay in the present moment. We all have our unique pasts that are colored with a plethora of experiences and emotions that make us who we are today, in the present. The issue comes when focusing on or placing judgement on the past - whether positive or negative - becomes a habit. But what of the future? We have wants, needs, and goals for the future; some are motivating, and some can be debilitating.
So, how? How can one focus solely on the present moment? It seems a mystery. The operative word here is *seems*. Something that is mysterious is fascinating, although

sometimes seemingly difficult to understand or explain at first. The key to unlocking the mystery of mindfulness is: YOU.

Usually, when a word is a mystery, your first instinct is to look it up. Learning more about how different texts define mindfulness can help you relate to how it will work in your life.

Webster's Dictionary:
Mindfulness:
1: the quality or state of being mindful

2: the practice of maintaining a nonjudgmental state of heightened or complete awareness of one's thoughts, emotions, or experiences on a moment-to-moment basis
also: such a state of awareness - *BINGO!*

Now we know how the Western Webster's Dictionary defines it, but mindfulness did not come into being when the dictionary finally penned it. Mindfulness is a practice that came from the East. From Hinduism first and then Buddhism thousands of years ago. In other words, the idea of mindfulness is old. The advice "respect your elders" most definitely applies here. When a word or concept might be unfamiliar, it is beneficial to be educated on the knowledge of its rich history; it can help reveal multiple perspectives to connect to.

A Little History

Mindfulness practice was born around 2300 BCE in Hinduism during a very tumultuous time. Hinduism is an accumulation of many different religions after a very complicated history.

It is important to know the origin of mindfulness because the ideas that stemmed from Hinduism, such as staying in the moment, emotional management, stress reduction, and a focused mind, are core values of the practice.

Principally, Yoga comes from Hinduism, which is a key that many people use to unlock the mystery of mindfulness. Before you take out your yoga mat, let's take a look at an essential piece of literature that gave the world a book to live by and study in the journey towards mindfulness and enlightenment.

A Hindu scripture, The **Bhagavad Gita or Gita**: the 6th book of the Mahabharata, is practically a thesis on mindfulness through dialogue while also being the first book of YOGA. (We will discuss the practice of yoga further in this chapter because it is one of the keys to unlocking the mystery of mindfulness for many people.) The Bhagavad Gita is a philosophical discussion between an Indian Prince Arjuna and Krishna, a Hindu deity. Krishna is commonly depicted as an attractive youth with blue skin playing a flute. Krishna is the God of Compassion and Love. Krishna is a perfect representation of a goal for mindfulness: to find compassion and love for yourself in the present moment. The epic poem speaks to many perspectives, including morality, metaphysicality, and spirituality. It's a deep read, but philosophically a page turner! It has been written and translated by others over the years and is available to read.

This quote from The Bhagavad Gita is the epitome to understanding mindfulness:

> *"A man must elevate himself by his own mind, not degrade himself. The mind is the friend of the conditioned soul, and his enemy as well. For him, who has conquered the mind, the mind is the best of friends; but for one who has failed to do so; his very mind will be the greatest enemy"*.- Bhagvad Gita 6.5-6.6, as translated by Swami Prabhupada

Allow your mind to become your friend. Sometimes it seems like there is a battle between you and your mind. Have you heard the idioms "love is a battlefield" and "the battlefield of the mind"? It is time to wave that white flag and find peace within your mind and love in yourself. Your mind tends to focus on negativity; future outcomes, overwhelming emotions or what you said to someone at lunch you know they took the wrong way. These thoughts can cause anxiety, depression, mood fluctuation and the worst for mindfulness, distraction. Remember, focusing the mind is the goal. We must break with the ties that lead to distraction. What a relief that will be!
The benefit of mindfulness is that you let go of the attachment to these thoughts and emotions. Let it go. You can do that with mental conditioning. Just like an athlete's conditioning for competition, the mind should be treated the same way so you can crush thought distortions and focus on the here and now. You have the power to train your mind to focus on the present. Befriend your mind instead of pulling out your sword and tearing it to pieces. You have the power to do this.

In Chapter 4: Control of the Soul, we will delve into ways to practice conquering those negative thoughts. This is part of the process of elevating yourself with your own mind. It's yours and yours alone. The relationship that you have with your best friend, the mind, is unique and it is a relationship that will bring you great love and compassion for yourself.

More History Please!

Buddha, also known as Siddhartha Gautama, is a master of mindfulness. Buddhists call mindfulness *Sati*, which translates to being fully aware in the moment, moment by moment, in the present. This led to the idea that the self is forever changing. Nothing is permanent, not even you. Buddha believes that mindfulness is the power to be rid of your mind's delusion.

The goal of the practice of mindfulness or *Sati* is enlightenment. In the perspective of the Buddha, as humans, we suffer. Once aware of what causes our suffering or what the source of our suffering is, we can reach enlightenment and freedom from the constraints that we put on ourselves. Say goodbye to your ego! It's for your benefit.

Sati is related to the *Zen Principles*. The Zen Principles have been translated and enumerated in many ways by a multitude of teachers and those who practice. Their significance is life changing and should be practiced daily. We will further discuss the many versions of The Zen Principles in the final chapter: Everyday Mindful Moments.

In the present, a monumental teacher of Buddhism is the honorable **Dalai Lama**. Time Magazine explored The Dalai Lama (formerly known as Lhamo Thondup and presently honored as Your Holiness), and names him "The Face of Buddhism." In today's world, consumed by complicated and dangerous political climates that he has experienced first-hand and rampant envious materialism, His Holiness is the epitome of love and compassion as he leads many a man and woman towards harmony and mindfulness through Buddhist traditions and principles.

Paths to Mindfulness

To reflect, mindfulness focuses on your attention, to stay in the present, be aware of only the here and now whilst releasing judgement and attachment. This is how we take in the wisdom garnered from our received knowledge through focused self-awareness without distraction. This is the key to reaching personal enlightenment in our individual experience so you can find your sense of passion and be compassionate to yourself.

An interesting misconception about mindfulness is that you need to be a part of a religion or cultural preference, and that has no truth in it. All you need is you, your focus, and to be present as you are, because who you are is perfect in the moment.

Human beings are all enigmatic and that is why mindfulness is a personal journey. There are many roads to travel in your journey to a life in harmony with mindfulness. Here are some keys to unlocking the mystery of mindfulness in your life. These are solid and specific examples of how you can take action while also examining the benefits of each. Find what best serves you and your development towards mindfulness.

Meditation

"When meditation is mastered,
The mind is unwavering like the
Flame of a lamp in a windless place.
In the still mind,
In the depths of meditation,
The Self reveals itself.
Beholding the Self
By means of the Self,
An aspirant knows the
Joy and peace of complete fulfillment.
Having attained that
Abiding joy beyond the senses,
Revealed in the stilled mind,
He never swerves from the eternal truth." - Bhagavad Gita

Meditation takes practice. We all know the sensations caused by being lost in a sea of thought. This allows you to see thoughts clearly, exactly as they are in the present. It is not an easy feat to quiet the mind and meditate, it takes repetition and practice. Once conquered, the possibilities for self-knowledge is infinite and almost dream-like. It will provide you with a sense of responsibility and safety as a gift for taking the actions that you will soon find are a necessity in your life.

Monks meditate all of the time! Now, I am not suggesting that you quit your job so that you can meditate all day and all night, but what is so rewarding is that you can meditate for minutes or you can meditate for hours. You can choose to sit in silence, listen to music or meditate while practicing Yoga or Tai Chi. There are also a plethora of guided meditations in various platforms and formats. There are multiple apps like Calm,

Headspace, YouTube, and many more that provide meditations in fruitful categories. There are ones for waking up, going to sleep, for anxiety, weight loss, depression, gratitude, shifting... the list is endless. Any topic that you can come up with you can find a meditation for.

The point here is to get deep. This is a way to become more self-aware. Meditation is taking time for yourself so that you can gain knowledge about who you are and what you are going through. Today's world moves so fast. When you are on the *go, go, go* all of the time it can feel like there is no time to breathe or to think. Meditation is time you take for yourself to calm down the breath with the goal to focus the mind. You get to inwardly pay attention to yourself. You choose to do that; you have the power to do that. It is the time to accept yourself for who you are in the moment. To be open to the fact that you are who you are and that that is enough. That is perfect for you now. You don't place judgement on what you are going through. You don't place judgement on how you feel. You let go of what you might be clinging to, you let go of what is not serving you so that you can focus on the here and now. It is detachment from materialism and the outside world. This is the time to find understanding in yourself in order to reach deep awareness. This is the time to give yourself some kindness.

With this practice some people experience beneficial improvements psychologically and even physiologically with the release of defense mechanisms that try to protect us, but which in the end are actually making us hide from ourselves. Your attitude can lean more towards positivity as opposed to the harsh criticism we place upon ourselves. Instead of being our worst critics we become our best friends. Best friends who can aid us in self-regulating. Best friends who can in practice relieve us from temporary suffering. Suffering can come in the forms of stress, depression, anxiety or another. That is why the Buddha and his descendants use this technique. Suffering decreases and positive consequences unfold with the practice of meditation.

On Meditation:

"Because all phenomena appear to exist in their own right, all of our ordinary perceptions are mistaken. Only when emptiness is directly realized during completely focused meditation is there no false appearance."

-Dalai Lama, His Holiness

One of the goals of the Dalai Lama is for you to get insight about yourself. Insight, or *Vipassana*, to see things as they really are in order to find awakening and enlightenment, which is basically the remedy for anything and everything who seeks love, compassion, inner connection, and awareness of who they are internally, along with the connection of the mind and body.

The Vipassana practice's goal is to discover how your physical senses, how you feel, see, hear, touch, and smell, link to your conscious mind and physical body. Once you have found these links through self-observation, purity from mental obscurities and judgement will float away to reveal a path of liberation and a higher level of awareness. The Buddha believed in Zen Meditation meaning here, to "just be." Sounds fun! Let's start with a story about the Buddha's experience with Meditating.

Buddha's First Meditation Experience:

Once upon a time, thousands of years ago, little Siddhartha was wandering around for many days and many nights until he came upon a tree. The tree beckoned Siddhartha to come to him. He told himself that he was going to sit under this very tree so that he could have all of the questions in his mind answered. He decided to do this no matter how long it took. That tree still stands today and Buddhists flock to witness it.

He sat in the lotus position and closed his eyes.

The Lotus Position (aka Padmasana): a cross legged seated position.

He started concentrating on his breathing.

This makes sense because if you are sitting in silence, the first thing that you notice your physical body does is breathe. Breathing is such a natural and involuntary thing that we do that happens to keep us alive. Yet, typically we do not focus on it even though it is of utmost importance. You are given the opportunity, the pleasure to listen to your own life force, with meditation.

He started to notice feelings come and he started to notice feelings go. He started seeing images of temptation, materialism, urges, and fear. The Buddha held steadfast, and he felt like he was floating. He was able to look at himself. He had had an out of body experience. He saw that he was reborn again and again.

Those are some pretty heavy revelations he had! So, he continued for seven weeks more, sitting in silence under that tree to fully realize and comprehend the vision that came to him. He felt different emotions; happiness, contentment, gratitude, purity, and peace for the first time in his entire life. He saw the colors that paint the Buddhist flag today and are symbolic for the emotions that he felt through meditation.

This is not to say that you should sit under a tree that will get famous after you sit there for seven weeks, have an out of body experience, and start seeing symbolic colors. That is not the promise here. People experience the benefits of meditation unique to their experience. Meditation practices can guide you to experience benefits that will be uniquely your own and help you find your truth.

What we can learn from the Buddha's meditation is that you will benefit by concentrating on your thoughts as they come into your mind and letting them go, not attaching and not placing judgement on these thoughts. This is not a time to become involved in a particular thought. Just become aware of them, accept them for what they are, and then let them pass just as a wave comes and goes from the shore.

There are many ways to meditate, but here are some examples to either get you started or to help you continue in your practice.

Meditation: A Practice to Commit To

The purpose of meditation is to find truth that lies in your mind to make you more aware of your inner being. We can reap the benefits of improving distracted attention, out of whack emotions, and the cognitive ability to help give you an alternate perspective on yourself. You can look forward to some fun self-discovery from reaching into the mind to step up to a higher level of awareness. And we know how important it is to keep our mind in tip top shape so that we can reach our full potential.

First things first, find a quiet area and remove distractions (phone, laptop, partner, cat, you get the idea...) from the room. Sit down with the spine of your back erect or lie down comfortably on a surface of your choice. Focus on your breathing. This is not the easiest task because our mind loves to distract us from noticing our breath even though it is good for you.

This is a small way to conquer the mind so that you can conquer it in bigger ways sooner rather than later. And what is great is that you can do this multiple times a day and this in itself is a form of meditation. It helps with quieting the mind and we all know that sometimes we need to quiet those voices down. Tell them "shh...." with your breath.

There are multiple breathing exercises that you can do to focus on your breath.

It's More Than Just Breathing!

Focus Breath

This is a very good place to start to become familiar with this practice and also a great spot to come back to because going back to the beginning is a refreshing place to be. Like most meditations, find a place that is quiet and remove anything that can distract you. Focus on your natural breathing first.

Further, you can alternate between deep breathing and your version of normal breathing. Notice how the stomach expands as you breathe. When taking a deep breath, inhale as much as you can. Hold for two seconds and then exhale everything, and when I say everything, I mean literally everything you've got. If you have ever learned anything about swimming and drowning, there is always breath that you didn't know you had. Try to exhale that out. Then hold and do it again. If you want, you can let out sound as you exhale in the form of a sigh or anything that feels natural and expelling to you. It should feel like a relief and should relax you.

What makes this exercise interesting is that you get to choose a focus word or a picture in your mind that will help you relax. For example, a deserted island - well that might be frightening - let's go with the beach, or the word "relax." You can choose anything you want, but it should put you in the mood to be relaxed. Make it something that is symbolic and pleasing so that you can come back to it whenever you want to, even if you are not doing breathing exercises. Inhale positivity and exhale negativity. This will help you let go of some pursuing thoughts. Let them be exhaled away like clouds floating high in the air, floating higher and higher until they vanish.

Breathing for the Equalizer

This one is quite simple. All of the counts of the breath are equal. So instead of inhaling and exhaling for whatever feels natural, you have the power to make the count. Just breathe in and out through the nose and count each inhale and exhale equally. You can decide to start with: Breathe In 1, 2, 3, 4, Pause. Breathe out 1, 2, 3, 4. Try to do this for five minutes.

Box Breathing

If you want, you can take breathing for the equalizer one step further. Inhale 1,2,3,4. Pause 1,2,3,4. Exhale 1,2,3,4 and Pause 1,2,3,4. You can make a box out of your breath!

Fun with Your Nose Breathing

This one sounds a little awkward, but the benefits feel pleasing. Use the thumb on your right hand to close your right nostril and inhale through the left nostril. Then you are going to close your left nostril with your pinkie and ring finger and exhale through the right nostril. Then you are going to inhale through that right nostril, close it once more, and exhale through the left nostril. You can then continue this pattern.

The Whistle Lover

If you love to whistle, then this exercise was made just for you!

First make sure you relax your neck and shoulders. You can tilt your head with your hand from side to side. Roll your head in circles to the left and then to the right. Raise your shoulders tall and tense for a few seconds and then release. Do this as many times as you want until you feel relaxed.

With your mouth closed, inhale through your nose for two seconds. It might feel weird at first, but you're doing it right! Then, form your mouth how you would if you were going to whistle. Even if you cannot whistle this will still work for you. Just purse your lips. Then exhale for five seconds.

Repeat for 2, 5, or more minutes.

You might want to aim for five, but if you can only focus or only have time for two, then that is perfect. What is amazing about this is you can do it anywhere. If people are around you, you might look a little silly to them, but what do they know? It doesn't matter, right? Because we don't place judgement on anything anyway.

Work Your Diaphragm Breathing

If you have a place where you can lie down and elevate your legs, then you can try this one on for size. What you are going to do is: lay on your back, bend your knees, and use a pillow to elevate your head. If you have ever had a music teacher, they might have made you do this to make sure you were breathing through your diaphragm, but if you are unfamiliar with this technique, it is very healthy because we are supposed to breathe through our diaphragm on a normal basis. This exercise will teach you how to know when you are doing so.

If you want, you can support your knees with a pillow or bolster as well. Now, place one of your hands atop your chest and the other slightly below your ribs. You are going to inhale through your nose, and when you do, you should feel your hand below your ribs rise with your stomach. Lastly, exhale, and tense the muscles in your stomach so that your hand stays where it was when you first inhaled. That is how you know you are breathing with your diaphragm. Once you are familiar with this sensation you can do this sitting or standing up.

Sitali Breathing: A Yoga Technique

This is a common practice while doing yoga, so might as well start it now if that is where your mindfulness journey is going to take you. Find a seated position, stick out and curve your tongue. If your tongue does not have that capability, you can use the form of your mouth when you would whistle. Inhale through your mouth and exhale through your nose. Continue to do this for 5 minutes.

Did you know that there were so many ways to breathe? Once you find your preferred breathing exercise or exercises, we can move onto different kinds of Meditation Techniques.

Meditation Techniques

Mindfulness Meditation

Once you have found your quiet area, lie down in a comfortable position. Focus on your breathing using one of these breath exercises, but instead, change the number that you are using to the count of 10.

Inhale for 10. Pause for 10. Exhale for 10. Now that you are comfortable, we are going to focus on the physical body as well. As you inhale, tense your body tight. Squeeze your face and purse your lips like you have taken a huge bite out of a lemon, clench your fists, point or squeeze your toes, stretch your legs out, tighten your arms close to your body. Then, release and relax.

Use your consciousness to make sure that every muscle and fiber in your being is completely relaxed as you exhale. As you focus on your body, notice where there might be tension and be aware and consciously relax it. For example, if your lower back is aching then maybe you can relax it by tucking your knees into your chest and rocking from side to side as you are exhaling. You will have the intuition to know what to do to relax the part of the body where you feel stressed. If during this a thought comes into your mind that wants to steal your focus, return your thoughts to your breathing. Maybe as you are breathing you think in your mind the words "inhale" and "exhale" as you are doing so.

Guided Meditation

Now that we live in the age of technology, we don't have to find someone to physically guide us through meditation. There are apps, streaming services, and podcasts for that! There is a whole new world of opportunity and you can find a guided meditation for any subject you desire. If you want to relieve anxiety, cope with depression, if you want to stop binge, emotional or overeating, a shift in mindset, to fall asleep, to wake up, to find gratitude, love, peace, serenity, the list goes on, and on, and on.... and on. You can find anything that you put your mind to. You can listen to it in the car, when you wake up, when you're doing yoga, on a break, during yoga. And there are guided meditations that range from minutes to multiple hours.

We don't have to meditate like the Buddha for seven weeks because we have other humans that can help guide us. This is very useful if being in silence is not serving your meditation needs, which should be to focus your mind on distractions. There are many guided meditations that focus solely on letting things go and removing attachment. There are meditations that focus on all kinds of human relationships. Some of them are synced to calming music as well.

Music Meditation

Musical therapy is all the rage nowadays. If sitting in silence isn't your gig, then music meditation can be a curing option. Music is known to heal stress and calm you physically without you being conscious of it.

Now, you can take moments to be conscious of it and appreciate it in this perspective. Plus, you have the power to pick your music. The go to for this is typically classical, but anything will do. With this choice you can do one of two things: you can use your power to choose music without lyrics so that you can primarily focus on relaxing, your breathing, and the opportunity to focus on mind engagement.

Alternatively, you can use your power to choose a song with lyrics. Music with slower tempos like new age or jazz tends to be more calming and apt for this session.

Basically, you are creating a musically guided meditation for yourself and if those beats happen to have lyrics that you want to meditate on, that get your groove on.

Body Scan:

Sometimes, just like our breath, we are too focused on what is going on in our pretty little heads to take note of how our physical body is feeling. Or we don't give ourselves the time to try to relieve some of the pain that we might be feeling or the parts of our body that happen to be tense.

How will you know when you need to go get a massage or grab a hug from someone if you don't check in with yourself? This can be practiced in the guided or unguided format. If you are doing a mental scan, you can do this consciously on your own or you can find a guided meditation that tells you what body part to focus on. Sometimes, at the beginning or end of a yoga session, the teacher guides the student through a body scan. This is performed from head to toe. It is suggested that you do this lying down, but you can do this sitting up or standing as well. Do whatever serves you. Each body part is given its moment. Basically, you can start with the head and travel down to your toes or start from the toes and climb up to your head.

For example, if you are beginning with your feet, you focus on the sensations you feel physically. If you are doing this, mentally ask yourself some questions: Are your feet cramped, tense or loose? If your feet are tense, then try flexing them up and down or back and forth. Maybe make them go in circles clockwise and counterclockwise. Make them tense for five seconds, relax for five seconds, and repeat a couple times until your feet feel happy. When you pay close attention, you can try to find a way to get a positive response so that you can be more comfortable. You do this for every part of the body.

Visualization: In the Mind's Eye

There are so many ways to get pictures nowadays. You can take them on your phone, upload them to your computer, post them on social media or even put them in a digital frame that moves. Visualization meditation gives you the opportunity to paint a picture in your mind to give you all the positive feels.

Opposingly, you can picture something or someone that you are questioning so that you can stop and pay attention to become aware of all the sensations that you are feeling. This will help in removing judgement. You come to this mediation as an observer to find your true perspective. Try to make the picture as detailed as possible. The goal is to not overthink. Do not overwhelm yourself; keep it light, effortless, and without attachment. Let whatever emotions flow (oh, they will!) and feel them grow larger inside. Allow them to become alive inside you. This can be quite challenging so commitment to being consistent will be the best bet to reap the multiple benefits from this transformational meditation.

We will talk about this a little more in Chapter 3: The Goal Getter in you.

Mantra Meditation

A Mantra is a word, phrase, or sentence that reflects your core values, motivates you, and inspires you. It can have any cause you want. If you are trying to not get back together with your ex, it could be "Don't call, text, leave a voicemail, like or love _____." It could be something that makes you more confident or more loving of yourself and of others. Some people even get tattoos of their mantras! You don't have to get a tattoo, but sometimes writing down your different mantras can be helpful so you can remember that whatever you chose once meant something to you and you became better for it.

Maybe your meditation became easier because of it. Maybe it inspired you to keep meditating. It can inspire you to exercise, eat healthy, and to be your best self. It could be anything! You can also do this at the beginning of any other meditation that you are performing so that you can feel more deeply relaxed. You can have a mantra that focuses on your breath. Just choose something that serves you for the moment. Find a relaxed position, close your eyes, focus on your breathing and on your personally formed mantra so you can pay attention and be inspired by the sensations mentally and physically that follow.

Transcendental Meditation

But First: A Brief History

Before describing how Transcendental Meditation is performed, it would be remiss to not spread a little love about what the Transcendentalism philosophy is and how it came about.

Transcendentalism is a 19th century philosophy from the school of American theology that focuses on self-sufficiency and, puts on a well-deserved pedestal, nature and how it influences the individual perspective. It stems from German Romanticism and both honor the benefit of having a spiritual experience. In 18th and 19th century Germany, a movement of intellectuals who valued nature, wit, humor, and philosophy made an impression on the Father of Transcendentalism: Ralph Waldo Emerson. Transcendentalism was the combination of artistic and spiritual ideals that were sparked by Germany and ancient Indian scripture. Ralph Waldo Emerson wrote an essay, *Self Reliance*, that details his position on the whole movement after his travels abroad. If you want to read it, awesome! If you don't want to read it in its depth and complexity, what you need to know is that Emerson honors the individual's perspective. He very fervently describes how society is too influential and judgmental on an individual, which leads them astray from their instincts and who they are internally and spiritually instead of blindly conformity to societal pressure. The goal is for the individual to build their own perspective despite what they might have learned thus far in the life that they have lived.

Back to Transcendental Meditation

Transcendental meditation is an extension to mantra meditation. Often abbreviated as T.M., this meditation has become very popular in the mainstream. Tom Brady, Hugh Jackman, Jerry Seinfeld, Howard Stern, and Ellen DeGeneres have told the world how much they love it. Because the subject is Transcendental Meditation, it does not matter what they think! What only matters is what you think about it. The reasoning for the love and compassion shared for this meditation that has practically renewed the movement that faded after the 19th century, is the calmness and clarity of mind, revived energy, utter happiness, and self-awareness that could potentially lead to self-actualization that can be gleaned from consistently practicing it every day. If you really want to get to know yourself, this is a good pathway to take so that you can make intentional choices on the day to day.

Are you ready to transcend? Take a relaxed seat and keep your eyes closed. It is not necessary to sit in the Lotus Pose or lay down, so you just decide how you would like to be in order to achieve a relaxed state of being. After this you are to focus on your mantra. Maybe it is the one from the mantra meditation, but maybe it is a different one. It is OK and perfect to have multiple mantras! There are just too many topics about yourself and life in general to not have more than one. When you think about yogis going, "homm," that is what we are talking about. It is a sound that vibrates and leads to relaxation. Sometimes your mantra can seem meaningless to you even though you chose it. Maybe your mind subconsciously gifted the mantra to you and it will reveal more about itself later on. It will take on a mind of its own, or your own! When a thought comes to your mind, accept it and then go back to focusing on your mantra. It is suggested to do this for 20 minutes twice a day.

There are a lot of teachers out there for free and there are teachings of this meditation that some decide to pay for. You can do it on your own, but if you want to invest in a reputable teacher, you won't be the only one. After practicing it for a good amount of time, you will be capable of doing it effectively everywhere on your own, but a guided teacher can help broaden your mind. Remember, there are a variety of sources to find a Transcendental guided meditation. Find what best works for you to transcend!

Chakra Meditation

If you have ever seen those images with people sitting in the lotus position and they look like a rainbow just shot through them, then you are familiar with Chakras. You might have heard about them in a yoga class as well. Chakra translates to "wheel" and comes to us from Ancient India just like some of the things that have been introduced thus far.

The wheel symbolizes that energy is circular (obviously) and is in constant motion. It moves through you cyclically like a wheel and has the quality of being a mode of transportation. Because they are located one on top of the other in the body you can think of them as spinning plates on a stick. I don't know if you have ever seen a man or a woman spin plates just on a stick, but it is marvelous to see! When thinking of the Chakras, it is a defining image: spinning plates that we hold together with energy. Look at what amazing magicians we can be with our own bodies! Where you get transported through this sensational process of recognizing chakras and how they relate to your awareness, reality, body and mind is mystical and sacred.

Knowing the location and placement of each chakra in the body is significant. Although different teachings might have slight variances on the locations of the chakras, this is a compilation of common ideas in order to get a feel for where they most likely are, what they signify, and how they connect with your body, mind, and how you relate to the world.

There are some theories that will mentionhow chakras are connected to the body's physical functions because of their location in the body, but these are not medical diagnoses of any kind. This information is something to be aware of just in case it does correlate, but that does not necessarily mean that it does. Remember, this is theoretical, but educational as well. It is hard to pin down forms of energy, but we do our best! Some believe there to be 114 different chakras, but there are 7 main chakras that we will energetically dive into now. Further, there are issues that can arise in yourself, and knowledge of how to alleviate the symptoms can be helpful to your journey towards awareness, mindfulness, and healing.

Root Chakra:

Also known as Maludhara (foundation), the root chakra is located between the pelvis and tailbone at the base of the spine. Its favorite color is red, and it symbolizes stability, grounding, and your sense of the big, wide world around you - when you feel "grounded," you can thank your root chakra. Because it needs to ground you, it is concerned with your basic needs for survival. It gives you support and a foundation for your life. It gives you a sense of self literally and metaphorically. The root chakra helps us understand our reality.

If you start feeling unbalanced from your root chakra you may experience disillusion, eating abnormalities (disorders), addiction, and insecurity from anxiety about your needs not being met for survival. It can be triggered by a physical or emotional trauma. Some experience just not feeling safe in their being. It might seem like there is not a reason for these feelings, but if you are more aware you can try to pin down why you feel unsafe or anxious in your current situation. If you feel inconsistent in your job, or are having trouble paying the rent, or you're nervous about a health issue, the root chakra is what needs some healing. The root chakra can exaggerate these feelings and make them feel bigger than they are. These can be feelings ranging from serious, like the ones listed above, to simple. Everyone feels emotions differently and uniquely.

To work on resolving the root chakra, doing something close to nature is promising. Get down to your "roots." Surround yourself in Mother Earth's colors. Try to access where you are physically so that you can maintain a balance and feeling of security. Yoga is a practice that will help your mind settle as you move your body on the ground using your own weight alone. More on that later.

Sacral Chakra:

Also known as Svadhisthana (her own abode), the sacral chakra is located above the pubic bone and below your belly button. Its favorite color is orange. It's time to get emotional and motivated! This chakra is all about your perception of your emotions. This is also the sexy chakra. So, if you want to reach deep into your emotional self (because we love feeling our emotions!), delve into your creativity, and get a bit sensual - then you are touching the sacral chakra. Some key topics involved that might seem obvious, but well worth mentioning, are relationships (we have them of all kinds), the sensations of the physical self, and loving behavior. Reach into the enjoyment of life with this endearing chakra. It is where humans get their instinct for nurturing each other. The sacral chakra helps you with self-esteem as you connect your thoughts with your emotions.

If you do not feel as if you are living in harmony with your sacral chakra, then you might have feelings of low self-worth and it may feel like you are internally imploding. It could be numbing. Those that might fall into codependency or overindulgence in delusion of desire in a sexual or love life can be led to giving into a false sense of emotion that can take you on a ride to nowhere. It is so difficult when you find yourself fantasizing about something that might not exist. It is time wasted on something that can be more motivating. So, don't get stuck in this mood!

You can enjoy new experiences with a new perspective as you really dig deep with meditation to get in touch with your emotions and how they relate to your reality. That is what chakra meditation is for. Find the motivation within yourself to search for why you are feeling a particular emotion. Make sure that you are rooted in reality. It is important for yourself to make sure that you remain independent. Awaken your sexuality in a healthy way. Positive affirmations like telling yourself "you are loved" will help you with your sense of self-worth. You are worthy.

Solar Plexus Chakra

Also known as Manipura (city of jewels), the solar plexus chakra is located in your tummy just above the belly button and right below the chest. Its favorite color is a radiant yellow and its focus is your confidence, your self-esteem. It is the chakra where the power of the self comes from. Physically, its focus is your digestion and your metabolism. A little obvious because it is centered in your stomach, but significant, nonetheless. This is where your mental capability gets to show its power! This is the instinct that we have where we feel like we have to take responsibility for our own lives. It is what makes us independent beings. To know your power is to know your identity and to feel on top of the world with who you are - who you really are after becoming more self-aware. With this chakra you assure yourself that you can be responsible, disciplined, make a plan, and confident in yourself and that you are amazingly relevant and present. To connect, this is where willpower can stem from. So, when we talk about being mindful, meditating, and finding willpower from within, think of the solar plexus chakra.

If you are having trouble finding momentum and inner drive, it could be an issue with not knowing what you truly and personally desire. Imbalance in the solar plexus chakra can lead to passivity and unwarranted peer pressure. This discord can make you want for a certain social status and false self-image. Yet, it can also lead to the exact opposite as well. Hence, the term imbalance. It just gets confused. When you feel that you are being over assertive, obsessive, helpless, inefficient, manipulative, and irresponsible, it may seem like your sense of purpose has left you, but it hasn't.

To regain that sense of personal power it is time to find a habit that makes you feel empowered in a real way. Journal so you can find what makes you want to get out and drive! Don't put pressure on yourself to be something that you are not. This is all about self-acceptance and the pursuit of a reality that is all your own. Balance is the answer here so that you can find a power that fuels you to become the best you.

Heart Chakra

Also known as Anahata (unstruck), the heart chakra is located in your chest, right by your heart. In yoga classes, they will tell you to place your hands like you are in prayer in your "heart's center." And that is right between the breasts. It is a special place and its favorite color is green. This chakra is all about unconditional love. It is the deeper sense of love where you find deep connection in all areas of your life. It is what makes you know that life is beautiful.

If anyone has ever asked the question "Where does love come from?" you can now answer that it comes from Anahata! When you feel forgiveness, acceptance and empathy, it is the heart chakra that makes it so easy to feel that transformation in yourself, for yourself or for others. It aids you when you are in grief, and gifts you with compassion. It is where your inner serenity and insight comes from.

When you have issues with weight, or high blood pressure, and even asthma, it can stem from the heart chakra. When you have an imbalance here you might feel jealousy, isolated, and you might have the instinct to withdraw from the ones you love instead of to embrace them. You lose that feeling of connectedness with each and all around you. The instinct is to get defensive, become the victim or in contrast the overzealous martyr, holding a grudge and becoming antisocial. Let's not do that!

To heal the heart chakra, it is time to find the love again. Start simple. Focus on someone who makes your heart start pouring with love. An unselfish love, an unconditional love. John Lennon said that "love and peace are eternal." It is time to put that breath work to work! Breathe in love and breathe out negativity. Breathe out what does not serve you in relation to the heart chakra. Think about old wounds and find compassion and forgiveness. Make a gratitude list. Say positive affirmations to the people you love and to yourself. Take a nice bath and focus on the things that you love about yourself. There are so many things, but sometimes in the moment, your conscious self does not believe them. Say it loud in the mirror and repeat. You will believe it and your heart chakra will be happy.

Throat Chakra

Also known as Visshuddha (purification), the throat chakra is located, you guessed it, in the throat by your thyroid at the center of the neck. It is connected to the neck and the shoulders. The throat chakra's favorite color is blue. This is the highway between our bodies and our beautiful head. This is the chakra that is all about expression. Express yourself! The focus on the throat chakra is communication. Our ability to communicate in all ways is indicative of who we are. What we say is important, words are important, and verbally is how this chakra expresses itself. Visshuddha's symbolism is very relevant here. When you are communicating you are purifying yourself of what you want to say. It is the action of getting your ideas and your emotions out into the world. It is how your verbal energy is expelled. Although it is verbal, it is also nonverbal, both internally and externally driven. It is how you communicate your purpose with your whole self and through the throat chakra.

An upset throat chakra can physically be susceptible to hormonal imbalances as it is very close to the thyroid. So when you are feeling particularly hormonal, or maybe you say things or do things at a seemingly inappropriate time, you might become secretive, or start telling lies; there might be a fear of speaking your truth, or the truth in general. Connecting with who you are internally to how you communicate externally is the goal.

Don't be small! Make sure that you express yourself and your truth! When fear of communicating controls you, you can lose your sense of purpose. Part of one's purpose is to verbalize with intention. In other words, be the person that means what they say and has a truthful reason to say it. Instead of taking over conversations for no reason, saying some gossip to a friend or saying something without being mindful, it is time to practice expressing yourself with intention. The idiom "think before you speak" is so key here. If you align yourself with what you want to say, with how you want to communicate yourself to the world then you will be having a spiritual experience that aligns you with your being.

Third Eye Chakra

Also known as Anja (perceiving), the third eye chakra is located a little above your eyebrows right between the eyes and its favorite color is indigo. It is that mystical third eye and sixth sense which dives into your intuition and provides insight into your mind and your brain on a spiritual level and while rooted in reality. It allows you to see all of the dimensions into the world and how they connect with you. To tap into it takes awareness that can be reached with focus and attention that will lead to comprehension. The third eye paints the 4D picture of your life and the world around you.

When you are feeling arbitrary in your daily life and feel like you are only seeing a singular path, or when you are fantasizing about a reality that is not your own, feel for that third eye and focus on this dimension first. If you are losing sight of the big picture, create a vision for yourself. Some even make a vision board to help the third eye focus on something picturesque, relaxing, and established. Try to find some clarity and begin to delve into your spirituality with meditation.

In Yoga they mention the third eye chakra so that you can focus on the duality within. We all have duality within us: good and evil, light and dark. It has been studied by philosophers, scientists, literary giants, psychologists, and individuals. Once one can notice the duality in yourself, you can perceive individual moments with duality in mind. You can question for example, if you are closer to the darkness or closer to the light in every experience. Yet, there are vast subjects that encompass duality because it simply means contrast, but it is complex and unique for every singular person. It is how you find and analyze your unique personality. Everyone is different and the third eye allows you to find your individuality. The third eye goes beyond consciousness. It's mystical!

Crown Chakra

Also known as Sahasrara (thousand petals), the crown chakra is located on the top of your magnificent head and is symbolized by a consciousness at a higher level. Its favorite color is royal purple. The crown chakra gets us to take care of business and that business is energy balance. The crown chakra is at the top of all of the chakras and takes in everything energetically that is being communicated from the root to the crown. We are all royalty with crowns so that we can feel wellness, serenity, and enlightenment. You can find and resonate with your ultimate purpose! The connection with your consciousness and your key to the most sacred wisdom is inside your crown chakra. It is right at the top of your head! It only takes for you to be present and aware.

The crown chakra is connected to the pituitary gland, hypothalamus, and thereby the endocrine system. The brain does take care of your whole nervous system, so the crown chakra is what gets all the feels from all the activity connected together. If you feel yourself imagining limitations for yourself and living in an odd paradoxical way, then you need to tune into your crown chakra. If you start closing your mind, living in your head instead of living the life you deserve or having obsessive thoughts about things that are beyond you and your control, then you are not allowing your crown chakra to thrive.

It's time to transcend! In order to connect with the crown chakra, find your favorite hobby that brings you peace. Give yourself a time to relax, meditate, do yoga, journal, draw, be by the pool, write a story or sit and look at the day or night's sky. Make sure that it is an activity that opens your mind to possibilities of your self-fulfillment. Be in a place where you can connect with your spirituality.

Back to Chakra Meditation

Now that we know what every chakra represents, we can get into the nitty gritty of how to meditate with this knowledge. We can recognize when a chakra might be imbalanced, and we can be aware of how they might affect the body physically (just in case!). The goal is balance, and what is beneficial is to cleanse your separate energies so you can feel clean and clear. Even though they are located in different places it is best to see them as you do your full body, as one full energetic system. When this knowledge becomes fully realized you can separately focus on each one!

Sit in a non-distracting area comfortably with your legs either straight in front of you or you can sit in the lotus position. Make those chakras upright and aligned with each other. Try to keep good posture, but not uncomfortably so; this is not finishing school, it's just meditation. So, take it easy. Place your hands on your knees and choose a style of breath work so that you can slow down your breathing and begin to focus internally. Try to remember the colors and visualize the colored rainbow of your body inside. Focus on the knowledge you have of each chakra and do a check in as you do a chakra scan. Check on each one.

Soon, with more recognition you will be sensitive to each chakra so that you can hear when one is crying out for some balance. You can begin to connect your emotions with the energetic physicality of your chakras. It is okay if you feel one chakra needs more attention than another. You may want to find different poses for each chakra. You might want to lay down to focus your attention on one, stand for another, and then sit down for another. Do what best serves you.

For your **root chakra,** focus on where you are sitting, laying or standing. Usually for the root chakra one sits down and plants themselves because that is where it is located. Ponder, do you feel anxious, do you feel safe in your environment? Do you feel safe in your life internally? If so, are these feelings appropriate for your reality? If you feel anxious use positive affirmations to make you feel grounded. Tell yourself that it is going to be okay. Think of something that lessens your specific anxiety. Think of something, someone or a place that makes you feel safe.

For your **sacral chakra,** ask yourself where your self-esteem lies. Make sure to check that you are thriving in your sense of creativity. Are you loving yourself to your fullest capacity? Find the love in your reality and in your relationships. If you feel that you are being fantastical and/or delusional in any aspect of your life, try to root yourself in reality that is respective of your love for yourself.

For your **solar plexus chakra,** find your drive. Reach within and think of where in your life you are already feeling momentum. Find where in your life you feel like you are powerful. Where does that power take you? If it is geared towards your purpose, then your solar plexus chakra is loving on you. If you can't find the power, reach deeper. Think of something that will make you smile so that you can be intentional in the actions that will move you towards self-esteem.

For your **heart chakra,** find the love for yourself. Place your hand(s) by your heart chakra or in prayer as a yogi would do. This is where you take all of your compassion, empathy, and unconditional love and place it upon yourself. Positive affirmations should ring in between your ears about how amazing you are and how good you are for others. It might just start with positive affirmations that you might not believe, but that is okay. Try to focus on one that you do believe and breathe on it. Find a mantra that reaches deep into your heart...chakra. Forgive yourself for anything that you blame yourself for and be grateful for where you are in life internally and externally.

For your **throat chakra,** think about things that you have said that really rang true to your being. What tactics did you use that you can applaud yourself for? Did you express an emotion in words well today? Did you hold your tongue appropriately and it made for a positive moment that made you feel like being nonverbal was the right way to go? Try to find how you were right and appropriate. If you were not, then focus on how to forgive yourself and how you could have made the moment better. Did you speak your truth today? If you did not, what was the truth that you wish was said? Say it to yourself. If you told a lie or if you were lying to yourself, tell yourself the truth. Be unapologetically you.

For your **third eye chakra,** make sure that your eyes are closed and focused on the one in between. Raise your eyes that are closed and focus on it. Think of your life as a big picture. Envision it. Start with reality. Start thinking about your day or if it is in the morning, the day that you want to have or the day before. Try to see it multidimensional. You can start with the plot of your life, then think about how you were physically, what you said, what you felt, how the emotions made you feel in your body, how your energy reflected from you and into the world, and then think about who you are in the world around you. Get spiritual. Think of your purpose. Think of what roots and grounds you, where your passions and motivations lie, your empathy, and your words and connect with everything else that you can think of that is you. Think of the full picture of every moment, every emotion, and think of how it relates to you spiritually: everything in you that is not material. Everything else.

For your **crown chakra,** think of literally all of the above and reach higher. After doing all of the above, think of reevaluating your purpose because it might be different from what you thought it was at the start. Make sure you are not putting any limitations on yourself by completely opening your mind and crown chakra and connect again to the immaterial.

Many of these connect with each other and it might seem a little repetitive because it is meant to be. All of these chakras connect with different parts of us and our humanity, our physicality or emotionality, and our spirituality that is with us through every moment and experience. You always take yourself with you and it is best when you have all of your chakras regularly balanced so that you can be mindful, well, and purified.

Vipassana Meditation

The goal of Vipassana meditation is to see things as they are in their truest form. Can you guess who began this meditation so the masses could reach its understanding? You guessed it! Centuries ago, Gotama Buddhga found that this is partly the answer to all healing.

If you are going for feeling freedom, this is definitely the meditation to dive into. It will clear your mind of mental distortions (and we know that our minds are all about that mental contorting). Be ready to feel as if clear air has gone between your ears, cleansed your brain, and set any illness that lurks in your mind free to roam the skies and be a blip in the universe. In reality, things that we think matter so much sometimes might be irrelevant a year from now. It might be irrelevant minutes from now.

This meditation helps relieve the tension that lies in the mind. This meditation gets you to look into yourself internally, like most do, but what is different about this is the focus on discipline. You have to pay focused attention with control in order to find the connections that discipline the mind. This is like a scientific examination that you get to do on yourself. How fun! We love science because you can learn so many interesting things in such a contextual way.

Let's go with you and this meditation being a science experiment. For your introduction: introduce yourself to yourself, but don't go too deep yet. You are the topic, and your life experience is your research. You have a conscious hypothesis of who you are. You know the general concept because you definitely have more than a first impression to base this on. The Vipassana Meditation is the experiment, and you are the results that will be exhibited to yourself. If you want, you can keep a journal as you go through the routine of this consistent science experiment. Take a step further and think as if you are having an out of body experience as you present the results to yourself.

This is a journey where you get to do some exploring into your mind and body. Feel the sensations and analyze them in a relaxing manner. Even though it is similar to science, there is no pressure. This is how we get to the root of who we are, how we think, how our thoughts make our body feel, how our judgements make our body feel. The Buddha believed that life consists of suffering, and it does. But how you are able to relieve yourself of that suffering is where the magic and freedom happens.

After going through the motions of this focus you will find that knowledge becomes love, and you will be more compassionate to yourself. Our body and mind need kindness, although consciously we are not constantly thinking "I need to be nicer to myself." So, meditation in general provides you with that time. All of the work that you do is to find a relationship with your body, mind, and spirit that you are generous to. It is a time where you can solely think about yourself. And when you are nice to yourself you build trust. With that trust comes more awareness, because when the body and mind connect deeply with consciousness, the subconscious sometimes decides to say hello and give insight to the subtext of your life. You will understand some underlying suffering that you did not know you were experiencing. Sometimes we put on a happy face so much that consciously we believe we are happy until we take a step back and realize that there is something beneath it. This is the time to rest and receive insight.

Now, how do we do this extraordinary life changing meditation? The meditation guide (could be you, a teacher, or another) will start off by having you focus on one object so that your other thoughts can melt away for the moment. Some examples could be a lit candle, a jewelry box or it can be something more abstract like your mantra, a song, and if you happen to be religious in any way then you can chant a prayer or visualize a figure of your choice. Anything that will give you a tranquil sensation that will give you the best scenario for concentration. The focus should completely change your mood and give your body the feeling of pure bliss - so think of something that gives you that feeling and find a way to harness it so that choice can become focal point. Your focal point is something you can always return to if your mind wanders. Just note that this feeling of bliss will not last forever and it is not supposed to, because then comes the next step.

Once that focus is felt wholly and completely, it is time for the next stage and that is to find reality. There are so many illusory thoughts that come up and twist our perspective, and we get taken away like a strong wind from what is real. It is like living in darkness because you are blinded by a perception that you have not delved into deep enough to know that there is actually a beautiful sunrise that is out of sight.

This is reminiscent of Plato's *Allegory of the Cave*. In Plato's allegory, there are prisoners that are shackled inside of a cave so all they know is their life within that cave. They are chained and all they can see is a wall because that is what they are forced to face. They know nothing other than the wall. A fire is lit behind them and they are able to see their dark shadows on the wall. They are able to see a form of themselves, but not their true selves. It is similar to us looking in the mirror. That mirror image is now us. It is an inspiration of ourselves, but cannot be touched, like our arms. No one has escaped this cave.

Finally, one person does break the shackles and goes towards the fire and is blinded because of its brightness. He looks at the wall and is in disbelief and fear. So much fear that he would go back to the life he was used to in chains, looking at the wall. The reality he knows. Although if someone were to drag him out of the cave the individual would feel so negatively - anger and panic - being brought out into the sun which would further burn his eyes. But, this fades.

Once released from the chains he begins to feel senses and enters a sensual world that he has never felt before. He can see the shadows now for what they are. He looks in the water and understands the concept of people seeing themselves. He returns to the cave, feeling a martyr, to tell of all he has seen, but now the darkness hurts his eyes as the sun did. It was oddly different going back for it was not like the journey it was to climb out.

The Buddha went through a similar experience with Vipassana meditation.

In this meditation we leave our imaginary world that we create for ourselves because it is the only thing that we see. We rediscover our senses and look at things like we had never seen them before because now they will be more different than ever, a completely different version. A different version of yourself is something you can look forward to as your perspective shifts. Some say this takes years, and it does. The more consistent and diligent this meditation, the more you will learn about yourself. But new moments of clarity can happen daily. As we learn to use our senses with more focus, mindfulness, and control, we can do so as well with our thoughts. You need to consciously find attention even when you think you are doing so already. You can always go deeper and one step further.

You will know what actually is. Not what you think *is*, but what *is*. You can step off the rollercoaster of life and train your mind and body to lean into discovery instead of judgement and attachment. A new attitude will form. There will be a new objectivity to you, and you will feel life in a new way. Being alive will be a new flowing experience and the unbelievability of that is astounding. Your mind won't have the mystical illusory power to play tricks on you any longer and it won't hold you back. When once you are trapped you will find the key and climb out of the cave.

Is this easy? No! But the rewards are great. Most things are not easy in life, but when you do something that you want to accomplish, the benefits are mind blowing. You will be training your mind so that it will blow in whatever direction you choose.

Qigong Meditation

Let's do some traveling shall we? Qigong (which is said like "cheeyong") Meditation of Eastern philosophy, hailing from the Chinese, provides a practice where the technique gets you to ride on the saddle of your mystical energies. It is time that we add some movement to the mix. Now is as good of a time as any. We have been breathing, sitting, laying down, focusing, staring at things, seeing rainbows in the form of chakras, visualizing outer body experiences, learning histories, and listening to stories. It is about time we start to meditate and move.

But first: fun with words!

Qi is actually not just a word, but a whole Chinese philosophy that explains the psychology of energy throughout the universe.

Britannica Translation:
Qi, (Chinese: "steam," "breath," "vital energy," "vital force," "material force," "matter-energy," "organic material energy," or "pneuma")

The Qi can be divided into different categories: Breath work, the diet and nutrition you create with the food you consume, your origin which relates to your nurturing from your elders (parents and/or guardians), your internal energy inside your body, your external energy that permits to the outside world, and the Qi that protects you from blockages. All of these energies combined make you who you are on the inside that is reflected and projected to the outer realm.

Yong can be translated to mean mastery, so our journey leads us to becoming the master of our own energies. There is not a solid goal here because this practice evolves your energies over time. This is not a practice where you reach a destination, but instead you honor the adventure to help with your overall health. Time to cultivate this experience.

The Chakras of China: 3 Energy Centers

Similar to chakras, Qigong has three energy centers within the body. In your lower abdomen, the energy also known as "jing" is the foundation. Because the jing is internal it is connected with the yin of the yin and yang. If you have ever seen the image of a circle that is colored with two different colors on either side separated by a squiggly line and two miniature circles with the opposite color of the opposite side of the circle, then you have seen the image of a yin yang. The goal is to learn how to maneuver the energy within our bodies in order to live a long and prosperous life by balancing our yin, our passivity, and yang, our activity.

The yin yang is an ancient Chinese philosophy that symbolizes the dualism inside us all. In other words, there are multiple areas in philosophy within us that contradict and yet are still connected and relate to each other. Examples of duality are good and evil or light and dark, hence the two colors of the picture of a yin yang. Jing, connected with the yin of a yin yang roots you and gives you a foundation both physically and internally because of its location in the body.

Close to the heart is the energy also known as "dan tian" and it is the storage unit for the energies that are qi that hold your internal organs and respiration systems balancing both yin and yang. Because of its location in the midsection of the body there is an even flow of energy both upwards and downwards. That is why the standing position with good posture in the exercises work.

Last of the energy centers is the Ajna, which is in the upper section of the body in the middle of your eyebrows. Remember the third eye? That is precisely where it is located, and it is the storage unit for our lovely consciousness because of its locale in the body. This qi flows all the way up into the universe through the heavens above and because it rises externally it is a representation of the yang in the yin yang.

Sit Up Straight! Relearning Your Posture:

This might not be like the posture you have learned previously. Regardless, the specific posture in Qigong is everything because it is the beginning of this practice physically. If your posture is not strong then your energies can be restricted. Correct posture will give your energies a clear path to flow. The postures do change every so often with the different motions and positions that you make, but there is a foundational posture to begin with so that you can have a range of relaxed and intense mystical moves.

Let's begin at the top with your beautiful head and shoulders. Remember that song "head, shoulders, knees, and toes?" We are going to go from the top to the bottom with childlike wonder as if we are learning this all over again. Sometimes we hold a lot of tension in our necks that shimmies and broadens throughout our shoulders and the bridge of our collar bone. Inhale and exhale while focusing on the stiffness of the neck. Use your spine for support and mindfully lengthen your neck and open your shoulders. Inhale and exhale once more.

Now that we are using our spine for support it deserves some focus. Take your finger and pretend that you are pulling an imaginary string out of your head. It is as if you are a puppet, but one that you have control of the strings. That will help straighten and uplift the spine. Look straight forward and pull the string. Try to envision the spine and its vertebrates. They should feel like they are one on top of the other. As you lengthen the spine this way you will feel the length and the openness.

Next, this might sound strange, but stick your tongue to the roof of your mouth. Once you do this you will begin to salivate, and that saliva is a powerful mechanism for Qigong. Don't worry, you most definitely swallow it, so don't choke now!

We move on to our arms from the shoulders down to the elbows. Just like we consider the three energies we are considering and focusing on sections of our physical body parts. Exactly how tension in your shoulders can go upwards to your neck and can go downwards through your arms and even the torso is affected by the stress. So, we have to get these flowing energies more relaxed. Start rolling your shoulders frontwards and when you feel that has served you start rolling them backwards. Visualize your anxious shoulders just plummeting to the floor, when in actuality, they really aren't. When you envision something in your mind, your body tends to follow.

Relaxing the shoulders is so significant to focusing on your back and your chest. Your back is the yellow brick road to your qi because it is the pathway to the brain and the rest of your body. It has a pretty important job. For this process to go swimmingly, the attention paid to the back and the chest is key. With you back in the right position you should feel that the vertebrates stack one on top of the other like the strongest of flag poles with a flag waving the symbol of your qi flying skyward to the heavens. This will feel right and you will feel a great sense of ease when doing anything in your life, including these exercises. To stack the vertebrates you are a pole, but also remember that the back holds wonder, this magical way of being very flexible. If you have ever done a backbend or a full wheel in yoga you really know what I mean! It can twist, turn, and bend.

So, the back can then be thought of as a rope or a string that connects at your tailbone and your head. The image of that is so extraordinary when you think about it isn't it? Try to do stretches that make your back feel open. Sort of like the cat and cow positions in yoga, curl your back in as if you were a cat stretching with its back held high and then bend it out and forward in the opposite way. Repeating those exercises either on all fours or standing can give you this sensation. Make sure that through this you are stable and balanced while maintaining straightness. Focus on your back only as opposed to moving other parts of your body along with it. You know when dancers segment their bodies to do specific moves. Pretend you are a background dancer to one of your favorite artists, work on these back moves so that the end result will be an open back and chest. Because when you are doing these exercises for the back, the chest is right in front of it and will file along accordingly. Once you do this for a little bit this will feel all natural and so good and liberating. The chest might have the natural inclination to sink it, but make sure that you adjust to remain upright. Make sure not to slouch!

Hip openers are just to die for. Sometimes they feel uncomfortable at first and the beneficial opening cannot be replicated. To open those hip flexors, there are many moves that you can do. You can sit cross legged and bend down so that your head can try to reach your feet. You can open your legs wide and bend down so that your arms touch the floor as you stretch down. Just be careful because this is not meant to be painful - only the good kind of pain that ends in opening. You can open your legs more than hip distance apart and sink down so that your hands can be in prayer position and have your arms by each knee so that you can stretch your legs open to open the hips. There are other yoga moves that you can do as well but listing them is endless. If you try some of these listed, you should feel the feeling of your hips singing in openness. That is the goal here and the bliss that will follow.

It is not necessarily instinctual to have fantastic Qigong posture. It takes effort, focus, and attention and multiple exercises so that your body feels open and strong. By now, after doing these movements to maintain Qigong posture, your body should feel warm, alert, and ready to get started and learn more. Any tensions that you might have had in specific parts of the body should be lessened and released. Once doing these exercises and then returning back to the correct posture you might feel some tension or some knots, but now you know how to give yourself relief. Finding the posture will give you the availability to find these areas in need. Sometimes we have pain, and we don't know where it is coming from, and now you will be able to segment your body and find the source so you can do your best to correct it. How do you correct it? You've got it if you thought: **Qigong**!

The Energy in Qigong

Pretty heavy stuff? Not really, because energy is light. Because we are working with energies, be aware that we are working with the intangible. It forms in our breath and we need energy to live. The word vital is repeated here and that strengthens the argument of how significant this is to our lives. How did we not know about this before if it is so important to us and how we are going to rejuvenate ourselves? The more we know the better. The knowledge of energies is a very spiritual tradition because it connects us with the universe as we find our place in the energies among us.

Science says that this meditation technique is a good idea because of its tender movements that give way to relaxation as this is a major form of stress relief, hence a way to cope with anxiety. Finding ways to cope with the feelings of anxiety are few and far between so we are so lucky to have found a key to that mystery box! Everyone knows that relaxation is healthy. Research has shown that this exercise and its various formations that the body moves through have been connected with the healing of our bones, our balance, and can lower blood sugar. The recommendation is to do this in the morning, to walk on strong bones, keep your balance (literally and metaphorically), and give you the inclination to eat healthy.

The movements in this meditation can range from relaxing meditation that is internal and spiritual, where your body is motionless and your mind is focused on qi, to full on martial arts. Although it might look easy, be ready for these exercises to be quite intense. Do not be fooled by the fact that this practice requires you to be slow. Those slow movements can be deceiving. It just depends on the video you are watching or the teacher that you go to.

A unique fact is that Qigong can be an exercise that you can do with someone else. If you are working with a teacher and you have some questions, it is best to just ask them. Fear not! Questions give you answers that will guide you towards productivity. Think of your body as a receiver. You need to listen for the airwaves and sometimes the teacher will give you a clear connection so that you don't have to bang on a TV or restart your router ten times like you are trying to get fast WiFi.

There are Qigong therapists who help you with affecting the flow of your energy as they help to heal you and improve function in your mind and body. As long as the purpose is to direct your Qi, then you will find Qigong to be very helpful mentally and most likely physically as well.

Breathing for Qigong

In Qigong posture, there is a particular way to breathe to optimize these exercises. Of course, just like breath work in general there are innumerable techniques, but this is a basic one to get your started. Some of the exercises that we have gone over before are a little forceful. This is meant to be more effortless and mindful, like the current of a wave. The wave might have force, but it is instinctual. Be ready to become your own breath guide.

You are going to be breathing through your stomach. Take an inhale through the nose so that you can feel your stomach and your arms expand. Focus on the expansion of your stomach and the opening of your lungs. When you exhale, feel the sensation of your stomach coming back into itself as your belly button reaches the back of the spine. Your internal organs should be smiling with glee by this point. With your deep-as-the-sea breath, your lungs will be swimming in oxygen as opposed to shallow, sandbar, chest breathing. Sometimes your bodily instinct will be to tense up but release the restriction and relax as you breathe.

To find this serene breath is not difficult because it is so natural. This the only task at hand at this point is to breathe slowly, with length, and evenness. Just like a wheel you will inhale and turn to your exhale and then exhale and turn back to your inhale. This is not to be done with force. You are an observer and if you do this often this can improve your breathing in your everyday life. If you are doing a strenuous workout this breath work may not work for you, but otherwise this is the place to start before you begin moving.

Qigong Standing Meditation

Not many meditations are in standing formation, but China gives great honor to doing so and many practice this standing meditation before doing any other movement in active Qigong. This is usually done for a solid five minutes and is a great foundational exercise. For a Qigong stance, make sure that your feet and legs are positioned either shoulder width apart or a little wider than that. Hold your hands gently right in front or your navel, or the previously defined *dan tian*. Your elbows and fingers should be bent and not stiff.

For the next stance, configure your hands to raise to your heart level in the midsection of your *dan tian*, keep your elbows gently bent and place your palms facing downwards towards the ground. In an alternate stance, begin to raise your hands frontwards by your eyebrows, or in other words the upper *dan tian* with your hands pointing away from you and out into the distance. Keep your elbows gently bent here as well.

You can do these standing meditations in one lengthy or short session or do other meditations with this one spaced in between them. You can do this for example: 5 minutes each position or do another meditations and 5 minutes of the standing Qigong meditation in between them. Weekly, you can increase the timing. Some people do this in up to an hour per day or more.

Just stay in tune with your body and do whatever serves you. It is suggested that this be practiced daily to maintain focus and balance in your daily life along with consistency in meditation.

Introverted Qigong

There is an active and passive way to practice Qigong, just like so many things in life. There is a passive and active voice in writing, communicating verbally, and taking action as well. The masters of Qigong especially enjoyed this passive action of meditation.

The two types of Qigong meditation are the entrance to the tranquil, *ru jing*, and the healing aspect using concentration and self-chosen visuals, *cun si*. When considering *ru jing*, the point of the matter is to become more aware, but without a specific goal in mind. There is no need to think about an exact place or moment of which to be aware. Awareness should happen organically. A goal that is intentional here might allow you to stray from whatever awareness might want to peak its head. A similar meditation to achieve this is Vipassana, which we have already discussed in detail. Both are geared towards focusing on the internal and releasing judgement.

On the other hand, *cun si* is the more interpretive and creative element and considered to be the pearl in the oyster. This is where you create visuals so that your mind and body can go on that journey with you. What a nugget of awesomeness! Visualization in the form of creating images in your mind or even on a vision board can be imperative to reaching concrete future goals, but for our purposes we are going to work on what our minds can do. It will feed on whatever you produce in the most amazing ways!

There are two variants to this passive Qigong meditation and the key difference is in your breath work. In the first variant, you inhale, hold your breath and then exhale, while in the latter you inhale, exhale, and then hold the breath. This difference is crucial as we know that breath work in any type of meditation can change the game. It is so interesting what holding your breath can do to your body in different positions and frameworks of the mind. Both of these passive exercises are appreciable to the body. Let's go inwards!

First things first, position yourself either sitting in a comfy chair or laying down on your back, and breathe with your belly like you were taught through your nose. Be sure to focus on the totality of your *dan tan* in the lowermost part. Remember diaphragmatic breathing? That is the direction in which we are going. Just breathe slowly and place your tongue atop the roof of your mouth as you lightly inhale. In your handsome head, breathe in and visualize the words: "I AM." You can visualize them in colorfully blocked letters, bold print, floating away like clouds, coming closer to you in their brilliance. This is an activity that really makes you focus on the fact that you are trying to become more self-aware.

When you reach the top of your breath after lightly inhaling all that you can, visualize "calm and" in your mind. This will help you relieve any tension. Sometimes we focus so hard on our breathing and doing things right that it can make us tense, but this is supposed to be done very lightly and calmly. That's when your body is going to be calling to you. "Calm and -" What??? Relax.

When you exhale, visualize the word "relax." Visualize the words "relax" lying on a couch, on a lounge chair at the beach or swimming in a pool. If you have done the math, then you will be breathing and going through the motions of visualizing "I am calm and relaxed." Do this at least 3 times in a row but remember to stick to that feeling of intuitiveness within you to know when you are ready to continue. If you want, you can continue to add words to the statement as you inhale and exhale as well. You can even change the phrase at the beginning to your liking. For instance, if you want to use "I am loved and safe" instead, you can use that. If you want to relax a certain part of the body, even an internal organ like the heart or the thyroid you can make a phrase that matches that purpose. The visualizations for calming yourself are limitless. To do the latter variant, just change the breath structure by shifting where you hold the breath. An ingenious idea is to use one of your mantras for this!

External Qigong

As a reminder, I said that this is where we are going to begin to get active. So, let's begin to activate ourselves through movements with our bodies. We are going to guide our qis with our bodies. Now that we know how to breathe and meditate using qigong practices, the next step is to take all of the knowledge that we have gleaned to understand how to manipulate our energies, and to move the body with all of this in mind.

The difference between Qigong and yoga is that in yoga, positions are held whereas in Qigong, your body is in constant movement. That will definitely keep you focused on the movement instead of trying to hold a difficult pose while you're shaking and wanting to go back to downward facing dog. Active Qigong is a fantastic way to get your day moving.

It will give you a sense of calm as you go through your day-to-day tasks and activity. Although this can be practiced with hundreds of people all doing the same movements at once, this is definitely a practice you can do on your own. But oh, can you picture hundreds of people in the background environment of a peaceful Chinese garden surrounded by trees with pink, purple, and white flowers, all doing Qigong in harmony with the same focus of calm and relaxation? Perhaps picture that if you are doing this solitary. The social aspect may speak to you as being with others does have a positive impact on your health. Qigong doesn't have as much popularity in our country, as much as yoga, but let's make this a thing! There are many exercises on YouTube and other platforms for you to become acquainted with the variety of movements.

Below are some physical exercises that are part of Qigong Active Practice.

To Release Anxiety: Arm Slams

Feeling a tad bit anxious? Time to bust a move! Take a seat, cross your legs, and place your arms tightly and closely to the sides of your body. Give them a bend like you are about to serve something, but your arms just won't move from their place. Take a deep inhale and make sure that you take all of the breath that you can into your diaphragm. Remember diaphragmatic breathing? To get all you can out of this exercise, breathing through your diaphragm is best. Quickly and with force, shoot your arms straight up to the sky like you are trying to grab onto the universe. Obviously, grabbing the universe is exhausting, so as you exhale with a deep sigh thrust your arms down to the ground and then back to first position by your sides. In relation to your Qi, this is grabbing energy from up above and then bringing it down to give you a solid foundation and make you feel grounded. This exercise should be done for at least 1 minute.

Ouch! My Lower Back!

If you are feeling tension in your lower back, then Qigong has moves for you. Not only does this aid in the reduction of lower back pain, but it helps with general circulation in the body, focusing on movements of the sides of the body.

Ready for some imaginary balancing moves? First, stand up straight. Then hold out your arm with your hand in the position of palm facing up. The goal is to keep very still, stiff, and stare straight into the energy field. Once you have that position, it's time to do the twist. You are going to twist your arm facing your body and then bend and reach over your head and hold. Usually in most exercises there is no twist, but the twist is the key here to make the side of the body long and get that circulation flowing. Do this again and again on both sides until you feel the blood flowing. Remember, the first part is important - hold your body steady as you twist.

Maelstrom Alternator

Something seems to be missing through this description of movement exercises. Now, what could it be? We have not worked our core into any of them yet.

With this movement, we are going to harness the Earth and link frequencies with it. Get in a standing position and take a look down at your feet to make sure that the width of the space between them is a little more than hip distance apart. You don't have to stand up completely straight, so give your knees a gentle bend. Pretend like you're holding the Earth right in front of you by holding your hands and arms out and making a large circle with them while you inhale and exhale as deeply as you can while integrating strength in your core. Make sure you are breathing through that diaphragm again!

You can do this exercise outside or inside, but this one particularly keeps you close to the Earth and nature when you are outside. It is so nice to have fun in the sun as your bare feet dig into Mother Nature's soft grounded dirt. This is particularly touching to the heart and that's why your circulation is positively influenced by this form of exercise. Improving your health is so important, and a priority should be placed upon this exercise. You do not have to have a particular goal in mind because the benefits occur organically. Qigong is not concerned with separate parts and categories of exercise but looks at exercise as a whole experience. This one experience and journey connects your energy to the Earth, to the sun, to other living things, and it gives you the ability to harness your energy through the movements. These are just a few of the possible benefits, but there are many more.

Sound Bath Meditation

Bath time! Everyone loves bath time. This is a little different though because this is all about the use of synthesia. Synthesia is when you stimulate the body with vibrations of sound. Get ready to see some colors! It is another tactic to relax the body and focus the mind. It might get a little trippy, but the point of this whole process is to take a trip to self-awareness and to relieve the stress that is manifesting in your life. Sometimes a synthesia activity can last as long as three hours, which might sound daunting, but it has the opposite effect. Many talk about how blissful and euphoric they feel after experiencing a sound bath.

So, if this is not an actual bath, then what is it? The word *bath* resonates, and it can be difficult to replace the idea with something that seems unconventional. Although this might sound like a New Age concept that would go along with detox diets and green juice, in actuality this is an ancient tradition that, just like many things that we have previously discussed, is thousands of years old. It's ancient!

Its origins span across multiple cultures and countries around the world. Those from Tibet have used singing bowls and the Australian aboriginals have used didgeridoos. Playing the didgeridoo can also have healing powers and requires a circular blowing technique, just in case you want to rush to your nearest music store.

Both of these methods have healing powers. Some benefits are that they help with sleep and stress because the music makes you laugh and makes you think in a productive way that helps reduce anxiety. If you go to a place where you find people that practice such rituals, like a spiritual ceremony or retreat, then you might see people playing a didgeridoo and using song bowls. This is just a heads up so you won't be surprised, and instead you can come with an open mind so you can be delighted. The sounds should affect your mind and emotions in a calming way. Along with the Tibetans and Australians,

Ancient Greece used sound vibrations to help anyone with a slightly disturbed mentality and with digestion. Music also has some physiological responses, like lowering blood pressure and the rate of your pulse and aids the metabolism while helping with digestion. Aristotle has written about how music from the flute is key to reaching the soul.

One thing that sound baths have in common with conventional baths is that they are both a cleansing agent. Both types of baths can be spiritual, and that is the focus of a sound bath: a cleansing of the spirit. There are many levels to experience a south bath. You know when they chant a mantra, or "om" at the end of a yoga class? That can be considered a south bath, but it is typically only a few minutes and sound baths can be as lengthy as a few hours.

The reason a sound bath has this name is because you are literally being bathed with sound. Picture lying down and visualize sound like water that washes over you. The curiosity is, what sounds can be considered cleansing for the soul? We already mentioned the flute and didgeridoos, but gongs, crystal or gemstone bowls that sing to you, cymbals, twinkling chimes, rattles like snakes, tuning forks or even a siren singing a song. Well, maybe they aren't literally sirens, but there are people that will sing for healing at one of these events. The powers of our voices can be quite mystical. It does not necessarily have to be a song that has lyrics or a song that you can tap your foot to either. There is a soothing aspect to the melody and the tone so that you can pleasantly bathe in it.

The results are breathtaking as your energy balances and shifts to a calm state of being. The reason for the music not being a typical song is because songs have choruses and stanzas that have a consistent beat, and the brain needs to be free of what it formerly knows. The point is for it to wander through a journey of the unknown in a safe way that is light and airy. To let go of the bonds that hold it together when listening to a casual song. And you can forget heavy metal! This is a different kind of release.

The difference between a sound bath and the rest of the meditation tools is that you need an outside source. Whether it be finding a class, a spiritual retreat or a healer, there obviously needs to be sound that is not coming from within. Just like when you sit in a tub and want water to engulf you, it is the same way with a sound bath. The sound is like metaphorical water that cleans your skin, but instead this is cleaning the body and the mind. While at a sound bath you lie down on your back. In yoga they call this savasanah and it is done at the end of the practice. Sometimes a yoga instructor will have some of these sound instruments and take you through a mini sound bath. There are certain classes that have both yoga and sound baths for extended periods of time.

It is so comfortable lying on your back that you feel as if you should lie down the whole time, and that is exactly what you do. Lying down is such a relaxing concept. Your whole-body weight is supported by the ground, your bed, your yoga mat, a fanciful rug or a tapestry. It is a nice feeling when you don't have to support your own weight. We carry it around all day whether we are sitting, standing, walking or running. We carry groceries, backpacks, a cute, clothed dog in a basket; so frequently we add weight to our bodies. It is nice to let go and let something else carry the weight for a while. This is a form of self-care that is so important. To be able to rely and trust something other than ourselves to help us with the chips on our shoulders.

Meeting other Meditators

The healer will guide you through the experience. Now, you are trusting another human to take you through a journey. The bond of human trust is a strength that cannot be replicated. This might be someone you have come to know or someone you don't know. The healer is good, wholly good. They want what is best for you for the moment. They want you to relax, let go, be cleansed and they know how to make that happen for you if you just trust in the process. If you are not alone, and you are at a spiritual retreat or other gathering that has a sound bath ceremony, you will find relaxation amongst more people. The comradery of people having the same goal - to do something positive for their mind and body - brings them together. Everyone is letting go of their materialistic life for a while to take care of themselves in this way, with the help of a healer. They first take you through some breath work which we are now accustomed to.

After that, it might seem a little silly at first, but there is some chanting, humming "om," and whispering mantras that can sing from this process. It is completely okay to giggle, because remember, laughter is part of healing. The idiom "laughter is the best medicine" rings true for sound bathing. As you are listening to the various sounds that float over you like bubbles, you should slip into a deep meditative state. Although laying down is the most typical way to do this there are those that decide to take some comfy pillows or cushions to sit on as well. When meditating in silence there are distractions, but in a sound bath you pay attention to the distraction, the music and the sounds, to guide you through meditation. There is meditation for everyone, and a sound bath hits on many different sound frequencies that get your brain to rest and your body to fully relax so that you can eventually recharge.

If you happen to be experiencing trauma, unbalanced chakras, an illness of some kind or a specific injury, there are ways to find a one-on-one therapist or healer that can take you through a guided sound bath meditation. It is theorized that sound bathing can help in these areas. Just like certain things that we have discussed before, it is not an exact science, but there are some who have experienced healing on different levels while continuing to immerse themselves in sound bathing. This experience is completely subjective and just like meditation in general, everyone experiences it differently. Everyone experiences spirituality in their own unique way. It is difficult to teach, but there are options out there that have worked for others and finding the right one that speaks or sings to you can eventually evolve and transform your life.

Yoga Meditation

We all knew this was coming. All of this hinting about history involving yoga, the Buddha sitting in the lotus position, and savasana at the end of a practice being a typical position of a sound bath, all leads to the same path: the experience of yoga and how it is a healthy form of meditation and exercise for mindfulness. What is opportune about yoga is that whether you are meditating or in movement your mind is focused.

Yoga is a meditative practice in itself. Meditation in yoga is translated as dhyana. There is a common misconception that yoga is solely a form of exercise, but in actuality that is not true. If anything, that is just on the surface, the cover of the book, where the subtext is crucial to understanding the meaning of the work as a whole. Yoga is the perfect compilation of breath work and movement that lends itself to a meditative practice. It's a true way to practice mindfulness.

It might seem like yoga is an outward study, but there is an essential inward component. As we look inward, we realize that our mind and our intelligence might not be the only concept to consider in our lives. The truth that we know about anything in the physical world through our experience is sometimes all that we can see because it is engrained in our perception and our minds. We have two eyes, and they show us what is physical and what lies ahead of us, but what about what the third eye knows? That does not mean you should stop relying on your perception and what you know. That still must be in use. Your vision of your life needs to mesh with what you further discover through your practice of meditation and yoga. Be open minded to what you do not know because then you can receive inner guidance that you have been deaf to as you were not conscious of it. You have to reach deeply from within and dig it out of your subconscious. That might require dulling your senses in order to find what is visceral. It is possible, it just might take some movement and meditation. That is where yoga comes into play.

In yoga, it takes great mental strength to meditate, but once consistently doing so a calmness will envelope daily life. There is a misnomer that meditation equals a psychic spectacle and phenomena. It most certainly happens to some people, but that is not always the case and just because that occurrence does not happen, does not mean that you are not meditating. That is why meditation is so uniquely done and how the effects pertain only to the individual. Plus, my version of a positive psychic breakthrough might not be yours at all. Everyone has their particular way of finding truth and light through meditation.

There are some practicing yoga who become closer to a higher being. The name does not matter because there is not a number for how many concepts there are for said being and yet, through yoga and meditation, some people happen to find that connection for themselves. There is a lightness to the idea of a higher being and when some are led astray to a darkened world, many find the light through meditation.

Again, this experience of finding that which is completely intangible is a personal plight. Some happen to experience it through yoga and meditation, but others are completely content without doing so. There should be no judgement attached to this. It is merely information. As long as you are making your greatest attempt, with your whole heart, to find love in the energy of the universe that is secure for you, you are on the right track. Using your emotions and your energy, acceptance of what is with humility and a sense of self surrender as you fully open your mind, you will find mental concentration that will lead to a focused yoga meditation that is balanced. Concentrate your will. We will dive deeper into how to do this in the future chapter about how to make will power your superpower. It all starts with concentration and focus.

In yoga meditation, your imagination does not have to be a tool for strength. The benefit is balance after forming a sense of peace for yourself. You do not have to be susceptible to anyone's influence, creating visualizations, making yourself foggy or being in a dream. This is not a form of escapism whatsoever. You do not abandon parts of yourself because that would be a form of disconnection, when yoga meditation is about connection. Stray from isolation. That is why yoga is typically done in a group setting.

For the benefit of managing worry and stress, meditation through yoga should be done almost daily. Doing it every so often is not going to produce the results that you desire. Focusing your mind will help you sift through your deep-set worries and other thoughts that are bothersome. Being present, *really* present, through the focus on quieting your thoughts, is what is going to help you stay in the moment for a true mind and body experience.

So, make sure that you set aside some time to make this habitual. Try to stay in the moment instead of concentrating on thoughts that can take you away from it. If your thoughts tend to gravitate towards the future or the past, try to let them go so you can place yourself in the present. The power of focusing on where you are in the present moment, where you are now during the meditation, will ground you and give you a solid foundation for your practice. Sometimes it is helpful to literally speak to yourself. *Where am I? I am in this room. Where is my body? I am laying on my yoga mat.*

To further help you to put this practice into action, do some breath work exercises or stare at a focal point (a candle, a spot on the wall, it could be anything really that gives you a calming sensation), and do your best to relax your body. Doing the above will release anxiety if you put your mind to it. If your body is feeling tense in certain places, try to move in a way that will loosen you up. Perform a body scan, that is part of meditation. This might take some gradual redirection from distractions as well such as background noises, feelings that sprout from inside or nagging. These are obsessive thoughts that want to pull you away from your purpose, but it is very possible to disregard all of them.

Take whatever drifts you offshore like a turbulent wave and keep the beach in sight so you can swim back. Just like the waves have the ability to push you back to the sand where your lounge chair is, you can control your mind with your will to come back to the moment and relax your body. That is why choosing a time of day where you are most likely not to be distracted is intelligent. During work when your coworkers might need you, or when your family might be geared to get in touch with you is most likely not a good time for meditation. Taking time out of your day is so significant for self-care, so let others know what you are doing to make it easier. Most people will understand, and if not, you do not have to explain it. Just create a boundary with them and say you need to take some time to be by yourself.

If you initially have any fears or desires, release them. Do not begin with any expectations. You do not need to desire a revelation or a fear of not gaining enough insight. With the effort that you put in, your mind will become healthy and strong. You are being courageous by beginning or continuing on this journey. It is not easy to make the decision to travel into the unknown twists and turns that your mind takes you on. Once your reach into these passages, there is no knowing where the mind can take you in order to find health and serenity.

To meditate before or after a yoga session, sit with good posture (we spoke in length about meditation's version of proper posture in a previous section if you want to take a moment to go back) or you might consider laying on your back in savasana. The yoga instructor, whether in person or on a video, will guide you. It is interesting that different teachers have their own way of meditating and they share that with you so you can experience what they have.

Finding a Teacher

There is a website called doyogawithme and they have a variety of teachers that work on different topics and different levels. There are many websites out there and yoga studios to go to, and sorting through them is fun. Once you get a feel for which one you prefer you can keep going there or you can switch it up for variety. Then, you can continue to do it on your own if you like. In the pandemic, many people are deciding to do just that, although some businesses are opening back up with lots of precautionary measures. If you are reading this post-pandemic then you will now understand the lengths that we have to go through, but the opportunity to meditate through yoga is not lost. Many studios have created online videos to support their clientele. They know how important it is to continue in the practice and sometimes you just fall in love with some of the teachers because you get to know them and their lifestyle of meditation.

The yoga teachers know that they are taking you for a very personal ride to discover the self and they do not take that lightly. They have been trained to do so and what they do is always remarkable to behold. They will help you with your posture when you meditate, and they will guide you with their voice and sometimes calming music so you can be in the best state of mind to do yoga. Meditation does not end sitting or lying down. Some start the practice with both sitting and lying down, some start in a seated position and some begin lying down, while some teachers do a combination of the two while guiding you. Some might take you through a chakra meditation at the end and some do their own thing.

When they start at the beginning, after they take you through a brief meditation where you will set your attention and intention, you will begin the process of warming up your body and starting the movement section. In this next subsection, different types of yoga will be described because they are all quite diverse and have unique purposes.

Yoga

Once you buy your favorite color yoga mat, you are ready to embark on the health-optimizing exercise that is yoga. Picking out yoga gear is always a stylish and a fun way for you to connect with yourself. Usually yoga is done barefoot, but there are special socks with grips that you can buy so that you are not slipping and sliding on the mat. If you have not done yoga before you will see that as you sweat the mat might not firmly hold, and yoga requires great balance. When you are picking out attire make sure you choose clothing that is comfortable and unrestrictive. Yoga mats come in different materials so you will find one that is right for you once you begin your practice. If one is not serving you then try to find one that would be better. Don't forget hygiene! You will be working out on this mat and just like you clean your gym clothes, your yoga mat is no different! Antibacterial wipes work really well and do not damage the mat.

Get ready to be instantly hooked by this awesome world! If you are already hooked, then enjoy the reinterpretation of a practice that is so close to the hearts, bodies, minds, and spirits of so many. You can be any shape, size, fitness level, and age. Yoga is literally for everyone. That is what makes it so universal. It is practiced in almost every country around the world. It can take the ache out of your joints, relax you, strengthen your muscles, stretch your muscles, aid you with your balance, relieve back pain, stress, depression, calm down your breath (breath work powers!), make you more mindful (and we definitely know some tactics to become more mindful now), and help you become more aware of your body's inclinations. Sing in tune to your body with the awesomeness that is yoga.

For those new to yoga, it is not just a form of excellent exercise. It is so much more than that. It's breath work, it's meditation, and physical movements all in one. Speaking of the movements, some of them are twisty, curvy, and might be difficult. If something hurts, STOP! You do not have to look at the person on the mat next to you and compete with this. This is just for you and you do not have to do everything that everyone else is doing if you are not ready. Some bodies can do things that other bodies can't. Some moves are better for injuries and some are not. There is no judgement.

There will be props in some classes! Everyone loves props. Blankets, blocks, straps, chairs, pillows, bolsters, and more can be involved. Different teachers use different props. If you are at home you might need to purchase these props or some moves you can just adjust, pivot or do a different pose entirely. Again, this is your practice. If you are in person, some classes provide these props and others you have to bring them with you.

Be aware that you are going to hear words in a different language: Sanskrit. Many yoga poses will be said in English or Sanskrit, but you will get yourselves acquainted with them and, because Yoga is repetitious, this will be an easy and fun task. Many activities use jargon, like dance for example. As you go from move to move in a combination of both languages, you will be reminded to focus on your breath, scan your body, and continually connect your mind with your body.

Most of the poses are done with both sides of your body. If you do a set of poses for the right side of the body, you will be doing so for the left as well. Sometimes your right side can do something better than your left. Sometimes there is more tension on one side of the body than the other. You will continually scan your body to navigate how you perform your postures, and remember, if something hurts, don't do it - try a variation instead. You can always ask your yoga instructor for a variant.

If you have an injury, let the instructor know beforehand so they can guide you. Breathing will definitely help you move through your poses and that is why the instructor will remind you to do so. You wouldn't think that we need reminding, but it is typical to do so when practicing yoga. Oftentimes, you do not even realize you are not breathing. In our day-to-day life we don't focus on the fact that we are continuously breathing! Yet, breathing in yoga helps you meditate, reflect on your day, and physically move from pose to pose. Try to breathe through your diaphragm like we learned before. A yoga teacher might tell you to tense certain muscles and then release. The postures give way to this as well.

And now, for some history...

The Ancient Practice of Yoga's Modernization

We learned previously that Yoga is an ancient Indian tradition but let us get a little more specific. Yoga, much like literature, began as an oral tradition, which is why pinpointing its exact point of origination is not one hundred percent. That is okay though, because most great things begin this way! There is something secretly mysterious about yoga's teachings. We know that they come from sacred Indian texts, but they were written on leaves! Even the best writers and scripters had difficulty keeping intact these original pieces of old school paper. Most scholars believe that Yoga was created about 10,000 to 5,000 years ago. So, that's a generalized idea that we have to work with.

Although we do not have a concrete time, we can narrow it down to its original civilization. The Indus-Sarasvati mentioned yoga in their text the Rig Veda. That ancient text is also where the concept of mantras come from. We can thank the Brahmans and Vedic priests for those wonderful nuggets. The development of yoga therefore was manifested by the Brahmans. Another stellar group of people who placed their hands in the yoga deck were the Rishis. That is translated to mean *mystic seers*. If you have ever practiced yoga before, you understand the mysticism in its tone. We listed all of the possible benefits that yoga has to offer and somehow, someway, the Rishis were able to understand this. The Bhagavad Gita contains the majority of the Yoga scriptures and those are most of what we know today in the modern world.

On a side note, in the Upanishads, there are 200 scriptures, and the idea is set forth that there is a sacrifice that individuals must make and absolutely internalize. This ritualistic sacrifice is that of the ego. You do this by gaining self-knowledge, taking action with that knowledge, and by doing this you gain wisdom. The word yoga continues to pop up. Action is translated to karma yoga and wisdom is translated to jnana yoga. We will definitely discuss the self and the ego in a later chapter because those concepts are more complicated than they might seem. What is important is that the action and internalization of your yoga practice is a key part to this sacrifice.

The oldest school of yoga, the classical age of yoga, is a combination of monumental ideas, crucial beliefs, and fun practices. Sometimes these ideas do not agree with one another, but the arguments are all fair play! Raja Yoga was yoga's first show and debut, and the showman was Patanjali's

Yoga-Sûtras. Just like we have multiple limbs on our bodies, the greatest showman considered there to be eight limbs of yoga. These are the steps on the ladder towards enlightenment. They were really keen on enlightenment back in the day. And hey! We all want to reach enlightenment, and there are so many dimensions to that goal and that purpose's journey looks different for every unique individual. Finding commonalities is helpful, and again, yoga comes to save the day.

As we move forward a couple of centuries, the depth of the yoga practice revealed more components that became highlighted. Enlightenment is cool, but what about the life we are actually living? Enlightenment is an idea, a destination, but the journey is the ride that we need to focus on right now. When thinking of the here and now, when we try to just take a moment and think of where we are, what we are, and who we are, there is something that is always there. It is our body. Because it is always going to be with us, we need to make sure that it lives a long and healthy life, because without our body the rest is intangible. Our body is something that is definitely tangible. It is what we know. We know what lies in the physical dimensions of our world and our body is our own. And guess what! Our bodies are a path to enlightenment, so everything works out. This is where Tantra Yoga came into play. Tantra yoga was a radical idea in its time, and it transitions yoga into our modern age with Hatha Yoga, the yoga we know best on the Western front.

But how did it get here? The plethora of yoga teachers began to be westward bound around the 1800s and 1900s. Yoga's popularity started gaining followers because flocks of people began attending the classes that were being presented and offered. What became blatantly noticeable was how universal yoga was. It had something rare that many other things in the world did not have. There was no discrimination. Anyone and everyone can do yoga; yoga accepts everyone. In the 1920s and 1930s the yogis Swami, Krishnamacharya, and others began teaching Hatha Yoga in India. After that, a mystical yogi master, Indra Devi, who learned from her predecessors, came to Hollywood and opened a studio. And the rest is history.

Yoga has truly transformed and branched out over the years. Knowing the history is helpful because it displays the evolution of yoga. If you want to do the more traditional style, you will seek that type of class out. Different branches of yoga have their own focuses and their own intricacies. You don't have to stick to one type either. You can cycle them, you can find a studio you love and stick to one, you can mix it up; the options are endless. Here are some of the plentiful options to choose from along with some little extras.

Tantra Yoga

It its ancient time, Tantra yoga became a modern development. What an unorthodox concept! Tantra yoga came about when teachers decided to break away from the Vedics. Sometimes, rebelling from your teachers is a great way to open your wings and fly. These teachers doing so helped so many people become one with their bodies and one with the universe. We all want to connect with the cosmos, right? A lot of yoga focuses on the outside experience, especially the ancient kind. It was all about poses and body movement techniques and a smidge less focused on what was going on internally. In Tantra yoga, the body is the flashlight in our toolbox that lets us become explorers. Instead of yoga solely being a healer of the physical body's suffering, to detach from those ailments, Tantra points its flashlights towards being more aware.

Tantra: the meaning, like the development of many words, especially translations, has changed over time. Tantra has been thought to mean *weave, loom, device, technique, method*, and more. These words definitely connect to its inception and its goals. Tantra yoga is a way of interlocking ideas. The rebels came up with a new methodology from the Vedas, created their own techniques with differing ideologies, and thought of the device, our bodies, in a completely different way from their predecessors. The body became a different tool with different functions. Let's pull the word apart - *tan* is profound. It is amazingness, greatness, knowledge, all rolled into one. *Tra* is freedom and liberation. Add yoga to that and you get an incredible sense of knowledge that will give you multiple aspects of freedom through various tactics.

Putting together sincere mantras, meditations, organic visualizations, and more brings us to the universe that is our bodies. The inner universe is vast and requires some seeking to connect with. To do that, Tantra yoga wants you to find kundalini energy in order to connect to our chakras. There is a form of kundalini yoga that we will discuss next. To put it plainly, kundalini energy is our spiritual fuel, but it's inactive. It is guarded. There are so many parts of us that are guarded and some for good reason. Our body's defense mechanisms guard us for the benefit of our survival. Sometimes, they do their job too well and we need to manage them and find openness.

What is the name of this entrance that our guard is blocking? The wonderful golden gate of our world is called sunsunma. Our life force, our whole word is prana. It is the ultimate in intangible energies, but it is the force behind everything: everything that we are, everything that we do, our actions and behaviors, and all of the physical processes that bodies go through that we don't think about. Understanding all of these entities is the goal of multiple forms of yoga.

Picture the sunsunma as an entranceway to the highway through the body's chakras. Practicing kundalini is imperative through yoga because it is cosmic and we want to connect to the cosmos, yes? Enlightenment is found partially through focused concentration and sincere meditation. That is the classic path. The tantric way is getting to your kundalini energy by breathing through the sunsumna that is being obstructed by our guard so that our precious prana can flow.

Prana

Prana is translated to mean "life force energy." This energy is absolutely vital for life. It is love, it is breath, it is spirit, it is life! Generically, yogis use this term to communicate how our energies interact with the universe and the cosmos.

Part of yoga is trying to connect with our personal energies, but there is an ideology that is common in yoga - our energies are connected with the energies of everything; and when I say everything, I mean EVERYTHING. Us, you, the planets, the stars, the sun, the moon, the sky, the heavens, our brothers, and our sisters, to some, are considered to be all connected. Prana is the original power, and it is inside of all of us. We are all made of stardust. When you are practicing, having this idea in mind can be transformative. Our breath work is how we begin to develop our prana. That is the base level, the beginning, and it reaches as high as our consciousness. Of course, our body is what lies in the middle of it all and becomes actively involved.

Prana's purpose is to regulate our body to help it function. Our delicate breath, core digestion, the gushing flow of our blood, and even our cells. Our life force needs healing just like our physical bodies, just like our minds, and just like our spirits. Some work out vehemently at the gym, seek out talk therapy, and pray habitually. Just like you can find ways to heal your body, mind, and spirit, and of course there are innumerable options of ways to do those healing practices, but the point is, our prana needs scheduled healing. Setting aside time to cleanse your life force is time well spent! For your own wellness, you would be sourcing your energy through your body and doing that through the quality of your energy channels, your aligned chakras. Once the pure quality of your prana starts at the base and rises to the crown chakra, your thoughts will be impacted by prana. That process will align your life force with your mind and your body, making for a life of great internal integrity.

But WHY? Why does this matter at all? Sure, I have a life force inside of me, I can groove with that… but is it really important? There are some things that just, well, are. Is there any significance to being conscious of it?

You might be thinking these things. It is important for tangible reasons even though it is an abstract concept especially, concerning yoga. One of the main points of yoga is to change the energy from within the body. You can change your emotions, your spirituality, your mentality, and your physical body, right? In the same way, you can change the positioning of your life force, your prana.

As you are moving through your yoga poses, your prana adjusts just like your body does, which will guide the alignment of both. Prana guides your mentality and produces your strength as your body goes through the motions of shifting poses. It also will give you feedback in the form of bodily sensation. If you are shaking while performing some asanas, you can thank your prana. Don't worry, it is a good thing. Unless it hurts. Then, your prana will tell you to back off. It tells you when to step back and heal for your own wellbeing. Most significantly, it is the core foundation of your pranayama, your breath work, which is the heartbeat of yoga. Prana also makes you super aware of the here and now, the present moment, thus, completely encapsulating your mentality. When you meditate, give gratitude to prana: your guide and life source.

If you are an advanced yoga student, your teachers might have taught you about how prana manifests itself through a yoga practice. If you are not, we are going to get you up to speed so you can be a stellar student once this might be formally taught to you. Prana has categorized subtopics called vayus; the translation is wind. Just as the wind breezes and directs the leaves where to go, prana directs energy through your body. Kundalini, as previously discussed, is the energy that is chilling at the base of the spine. This is the energy we want to awaken during yoga, so you tell your prana to wake that baby up! Shakti is the universal energy of our own bodies surrounded by our environment. This is connected to Shiva who is the beholder of all consciousness.

Whatever we consume is how prana flows through the body. The food we eat and the beautiful air we inhale is us living, eating, and breathing the universe and the stars above. The minute channels it travels through, or nadis, is how it goes through every cell contained in the body. Our three main nadis are pigala, ida, and sushuma and they start from the base of the spine to the tops of our heavenly heads.

The pingala and ida braid through each other and gracefully rainbow upwards towards our nostrils as the sushuma arches straight up the spine to the crown of our heads. Our chakras are elongated at the criss-cross of the ida and pingala. Those meet with the sushuma. See? Everything is connected! The chakras and the nadis create one copacetic prana family. The key here is that the sushama links the prana to each chakra and that process blocks the kundalini from gradually moving upwards and protruding into the sushuma and then to the crown of your beautiful head.

A way to visualize prana is to feel how your body's sensations change with your posture. For example, if you are slouching, shoulders hunched, back curved forwards, head and neck turned downwards, then your prana will be weakened. Your chakras are not aligned the way that they are supposed to be and that is restricting of your energy. You will even find breath work to be more challenging.

If you are upright, posture straight, whether sitting or standing, your chakras will be aligned, and your energy will flow more smoothly. Your breath will control your prana. As you inhale the energy shoots upwards to the stars and when you exhale your energy is falling freely to your toes. Recognizing how to manipulate your prana to your liking will help you consciously. Your concentration will be at an all-time high.

Our Vrittis

The yogi's perspective on how our thoughts work is translated to chitta vritti. We have some vrittis that we are extremely conscious of and there are some that are hiding in the darkness. Trust in the fact that with practice we can find the light. Knowledge of the vrittis is the first step, because once we know that they exist, we can delve deeper into the comprehension of them and how we can access our inner thoughts.

There are painful vrittis, translated as klishta, and non-painful vrittis, translated to mean aklishta. There is accurate perception, everything we actually know because we have seen it; delusion, things that have been miscommunicated by us leading us to a false reality; imagination, our fantastical fantasies and possibly delusions of grandeur, when we are sleeping, our thoughts during a lack of consciousness phase; and our memories, what we can recollect through our past thoughts, emotions, life events and experiences. As you meditate through yoga, keep these in mind as your thoughts come and go. You can decipher which vritti is being accessed.

The practice of yoga calms the mind and therefore, our life experience in that moment. So technically, if you can control your prana, you can have more control over your mind. With yoga, meditation is made more simple and with this process you become more in tune with yourself and with the universe.

5 Koshas

When you have the gained luxury of being aware of your prana, you will be able to manipulate the energies in your body. This is the awareness of Prayamana Kosha and the Koshas are the relevance of your True Self.

There are 5 koshas that swathe the True Self. The Ancient Ones, the yogis that came before us, basically created a treasure map so that we can look internally to find the nuggets of gold that is our True Self or are our Selves. Our selves, or atma, came to knowledge in the Upanishads, an ancient yogi text, so it is an old and reliable concept. It took centuries for Advaita Vedanta to figure it all out for us. Picture the koshas like layers of an onion. Our True Self lies in the center of that very onion and yoga is the knife that delicately, or sometimes not so delicately, slices those layers apart. In your practice, as the layers begin to fall off, you will become more aware. This allows you to move more deeply into discovering your True Self, your more inward core. Yoga is the sergeant that tells your koshas to get in line so that you can become one with yourself and the universe combined.

The skin of the onion is the physical body, our Annamaya Kosha. *Anna* is translated to be food, and that food needs to be eaten healthily so that you can reach the other four koshas, metaphorically speaking.

Once cleared of the Annamaya Kosha we can reach into our energetic body. The Pranamaya Kosha is our life, our force, our energy. Therefore, this is how we move. This is how we get our nadis and chakras to dance. The Manamaya Kosha is the inhabitants of our mind. This is the screen of our fun emotions and our awesome, and sometimes not so awesome, mentalities. We need to know it all though! The Manamaya Koash is where our thoughts come to be. The Vijnanamaya Kosha is the final layer, and it is our sense of knowledge, our wisdom. This is where our intuition comes from and how our conscious becomes our guide.

The Anandamaya Kosha is the True Self, our inherent bliss, or Ananda. It is unconditional love, pure bliss, and complete happiness. The ecstasy of the Anandamaya Kosha is unyielding. That is why it has the most depth in our being and it exists in us always. Just like Dorothy wants to be home and realizes she was there all along, and that she was just in a dream. Our dream is our life. We are always home. We can reach this state of bliss because it is always in us. We just have to go through the incredible journey of peeling off the other koshas from time to time and then we will reach it.

That is when you will be conscious of your True Self. It is most definitely an impactful life journey; an inward journey always is. That is why doing yoga helps you find your own individuality and identity. All of your koshas are unique to you and the practice of yoga brings awareness to this part of your nature.

Once you begin to advance your yoga practice you will go beyond just the physical movements of your body or your Annamaya Kosha. With your blissful breath work, you can breathe into your Pranamaya Kosha, thus connecting with the body through your breath. Your deep inhaling and exhaling whilst doing yoga movements will bring radiance to your mind and emotions. The Manayama Kosha will awaken you to the calmness and twinkling of your mind, but inadvertently your thoughts and their depth will lessen. This is when you will be able to seek your inner guide, the wisdom that fuels you that oftentimes you cannot hear or fully access. The Vinjinyamana Kosha's intuition will speak to you and balance you. Once completely fulfilling this sequence, it is said that you can potentially reach Enlightenment and be fully and completely one with yourself.

Pratyathara

The technique for delving into focusing inwards is pratyahara, which can be translated to mean the withdrawal of the senses. It is partly how we bring unity to our mind and our spirits. When you release your vision and focus on what is going on around you, then you are focusing on yourself. Once your focus diverts from your outer self, then you can focus on your inner self. Your breathing and physical sensations inside can become your concentration during yoga practices. This can bring understanding to your deepest fears, how you might limit yourself in your mind, and the expectations that you set in your mind.

The key here is detaching so you can look into a lens that is unbiased. It is like you are your best self, peering into a self that is similar to a best friend's. You become your own best friend who wants you to overcome your fears, release the limitations that you set in your mind, and let go of the expectations you might have. Through your body's movement and your breath work you use the sensations in your body to be more aware of these aspects of yourself. Just remember, be kind to yourself. Yes, this is a consistent discipline, but this is a worthwhile journey that takes compassion so that you can have full awareness of these topics that are typically blocked from you.

Connections to Tantra

As we come to the conclusion of our Tantra Yoga section, it is best to connect all of these ideas and why they matter. This is not a vocabulary test!

- Connecting our energies, our prana, and releasing our kundalini energy is the purpose of the physical practice of Tantra yoga.
- Breathing, awareness of our koshas, awareness of our vritis, and focusing on pratyahara will make our yoga asanas more meaningful and authentic.
- Create a mantra that is purposeful for your Tantra Yoga session.

This is not something that you will be doing all at once. This is a lot of information. Some of it will happen seamlessly and some might take more conscious awareness. Try to create a mantra that will help you concentrate on a specific aspect of Tantra. Maybe make a couple that will take you organically through your asanas.

As you become more disciplined, you will notice what movements might strike a way for you to find depth into one of the elements. Enjoy your journey! The benefit of self-awareness is a lengthy one, but an enlightened one!

Kundalini Yoga

Ready to feel the outer and inner bliss? Knowing traditional Hatha Yoga practices, the ones that are most common in the United States, the more physically involved, is the foundation for Kundalini Yoga - but these movements should be done in a specific order. This way the energies within you will become stronger.

Through asanas (traditional yoga poses) and pranayama (controlling your breath work to help control your mind), mudras (movements) and meditation, you are setting alarm clocks for your chakras. Once these tasks feel fulfilled in that moment, you can meet your kundalini. All of this can benefit you internally.

Once the highway of your passageways is clear, your chakras can hook up your consciousness and boom! Peace, serenity, improved cognitive function, self-awareness, increased perception, empathy, creativity, you might become more charismatic, your levels of energy will skyrocket, and more. Varying benefits are unique to every individual but some, if not all of these can become part of your journey if you include Kundalini yoga into your habitual regimen.

Do you like to sing? Chant maybe? If you answered yes to any of these questions, then Kundalini Yoga might be singing your name! Through chanting, singing, yoga poses, and breath work you can begin to activate your Kundalini energy, which begins to kindle its power at the base of your spine. Some yoga enthusiasts might also name Kundalini as the "yoga of awareness," but that seems a little like an umbrella term because all forms of yoga make you aware in one way or another. Another benefit to this practice is that it is a way of letting go of the ego. Again, we will be diving deeply into the philosophy and psychology of the ego in a later chapter.

We know of Kundalini yoga because it was mentioned in the Veda texts, but its actual origin is unknown, which is a little frustrating for us history nerds. What we do know is that "kunda" means circular. Just like the circle of life. Another interpretation is that it is like a coiled snake. The imagery is trying to impress that at the base of the spine there is a resting snake just hanging out. The spirit of the serpent is an ancient symbol for rebirth and transformative experiences which is why Kundalini is often connected with it. This snake is just waiting to be released to connect you to higher love and power!

A way that Kundalini differs from the vast other forms of yoga is that it is most definitely lighter on the body. The circular, repetitive motions concept is the same, but the focus is heavily on the spiritual side. The movements are also extremely condensed. A lot of yoga classes can have poses that are lengthy and last for minutes at a time, so this is quite the opposite and feels sensually relieving.

6 Phases of Kundalini

Once you get into a Kundalini class and settle in, you will be ready to begin. There are six phases in Kundalini yoga. Just like you would if you were about to play an instrument, you tune up, or in this case tune in. The class will start with a chant. It is so beautiful when a group of people, striving for the same goal of reaching their Kundalini energy, chant together. An energy just sweeps the room. That is the first phase. Once the chant is in decrescendo, the warm-up begins.

Phase two, or Prayamana, is where you begin to focus on your breath, or pranayama, and some movement geared towards your spine. Once you are in tune with your breath phase three starts to take form. You go through a series of brief movements. You might be told to get into certain postures, breathe, move your hands in specific positions also known as mudras (we will get into more detail in our Hatha Yoga section coming up next), and sounds might be involved in different forms as well. This phase is called Kriya. During Kriya is when the energies start to wake up - so much so that phase four is the relaxation phase. You get to relax and soak up all of that Kriya goodness.

The fifth phase is the meditation section. This is where you become more aware of everything you just evolved through. And to close the session, phase six is a closing chant. You might have been able to infer that one because kundalini does mean circular!

Hatha Yoga

The Hatha Yoga Pradipika was written by Swami Swatamarama around the 15th century CE in India. Swami's recognition is that we need to control the body, discipline the body, and consistently do this yoga practice in order to reach certain goals. He highlighted spiritual goals, control of the self, and well-rounded discipline. There are many more texts that dive into Hatha Yoga as well, so if you are inspired to go out and read some of them, they are readily available.

So, how did Hatha Yoga come to the United States for our delight? We can thank T. Krishnamacharya for traveling around India and teaching it to all who wanted knowledge of it. He would perform demonstrations that included different poses from what India had already popularly known. Many schools were created because of how wonderful it was and the United States finally got the call and answered! Now, we have Hatha Yoga.

Hatha is modern day yoga. It actually got its roots from Tantric yoga, hence the segue! This is one of the most traditionally taught yoga schools in the United States where they focus on the physical aspects. Now, tantric yoga is all about the physical body as a pathway towards enlightenment, while Hatha is a braid of the physical and the spiritual with the use of the bodily energetic fields. We are trying to purify and cleanse our minds and bodies here. This is the prerequisite for Raja Yoga, which is in the next segment.

"Ha" is symbolic for the sun and "tha" is symbolic for the moon. The symbolism of the imagery of the night and the day is a historic one indeed. It became a representation of the mind and body. The awareness of hatha yoga gives way to us singing to the tune of our body, spirit, and mind. We can continue with our metaphor all day and night. Pretend as if your body is an instrument, your energy is a song, and the music with or without lyrics flow into your mind.

Hatha yoga is taught using specific movement flows which are translated as asana, breathing which is translated to pranayama, and mudra which means body gestures. The ones concerning the whole body become asanas, while doing pranayama consistently, in order to awaken our prana: our bodily energy, our chakras, and our kundalini energy. Prana and kundalini are wonderful and engaging concepts. Let's begin with mudras.

Mudras have bodily concentrations, those being the face, hands, and then composing of the entire body.

Mudras

The purpose of mudras is that they awaken the eight powers of the divine. Our hands, our hastas, are principal aspects to meditation and are used in our asana practices and even in our daily lives as we develop our pranayama. As you put your hands in a prayer position against your back (I know that might feel a little funny at first) you can trace your fingers up and down your back. The benefit is that you are awakening your awareness of your mentality and your emotions.

Once your hands leave the prayer position you can travel your fingers up and down the spine. When you focus on the mudras of your head, you become awakened to your senses. Really focus on your eyes, nose, lips, your ears. Scan the senses of your head. What do you see? It is alright if your eyes are closed. Do you smell anything? Sometimes a yoga instructor might have incense or a diffuser going. If you are at home, you can buy a diffuser, light a candle or use essential oils to elevate your sense of smell. It can also create a calming, energetic, relaxed or even detoxed effect depending on how your body and mind react to the scent. Focus on how your head feels. Is it buzzing? Are your thoughts cycling? Do you want to shift your mind a tad?

Lastly, pay attention to your pelvis. Small movements will begin to awaken your prana and gear you towards sending it through your chakras to reach your kundalini energy.

Hatha Classes

Hatha yoga classes are very easy to find because now, Hatha yoga is practically generalized as Yoga. Basically, if you are going to go to a yoga class, this is most likely the yoga that you are going to encounter, and you will be lucky to have found it! Beginners and experienced alike are welcome. Hatha yoga is great for everyone, and especially for beginners who have just started to figure this whole thing out.

There will typically be a warm-up period, a sequence of yoga poses, and a restful period along with some breath work. Bonus if you know the Sanskrit terms for all of these terms in the process! The class can last up to 90 minutes and usually for as little as 60 minutes. A yoga structure will help you align your body to a correct pose. Throughout the class you will have moments where you feel a deep sense of relaxation, calmness, possible spiritual moments, emotional clarity, strength building, fun flexibility, and a rise in stamina. All of this and more will come as you switch from pose to pose with elegance.

Raja Yoga AKA Ashtanga Yoga

Get ready to work it out! Raja, also referred to as Ashtanga Yoga, is definitely a challenge, but challenges are the best way to grow. Raja can be translated to mean king. Let us think about the qualities of a king's greatness. A good king is independent, a free thinker, self-assured, and confident. Raja yoga is all about gaining independence, a sense of fearlessness, and of course, self-discipline. There are eight fun steps to Raja or Ashtanga yoga. Consider them an instruction manual to self-awareness, clarity, and self-control.

- Yama is your focus on self-control, and it is based on five significant principles. Ahimsa is translated to mean the nonviolent. We are not just speaking about a physical altercation. This means to not think, speak or take action negatively on any living thing. There is no need to cause any pain to anyone or anything. Even our thoughts can produce negativity. Our words most definitely have immense power, and we need to speak with intention and positivity.

- Satya is translated to mean truthfulness. In our words, we speak the truth. That does not mean to blurt out harsh words, because we can speak truth always with love.
- Asteya translates to non-stealing. We do not rob anyone of anything. We do not rob people of their reality (tell the truth), their property or their mentality.
- A pure way of life is the translation of Brahmacharya. That is indicative of our thoughts leaning consistently towards a higher purpose. It is to let go of the negativity that selfishness can bring. Of course, there are moments in life where we need self-care, but this principle refers to taking action, oftentimes for what your best self would think it best for you to do.
- Lastly, Aparigraha means to not take possession of anything that you do not need. This is the purest form of letting go of attachments, especially those that are materialistic. Doing this will provide a great sense of freedom.

Just like there are 5 principles to Yama there are also 5 principles to Niyama which can be translated to mean discipline.

- Shauca is our internal purity in spirit, in truth, and in all that is forthcoming in your life.

- Santosh is your sense of contentment and knowing the good in everything around us. That is a reminder to be compassionate with yourself and those around you.
- Tapa is our sense of self control. No matter what the challenge is that we are facing, know that you can overcome it with a controlling manner. Stay determined, live in patience, persevere no matter what, and practice, practice, practice.
- Swadhyaya is to study what is holy. The ancient ones were continuous and diligent in their studies of their texts just as we study in our schools. Consider yoga to be your ancient text.
- Ishvara Pranidhana is the devotion to what is higher. Some consider that a devotion to God, but that does not have to be the end all. There is a divine part of us that lies in ourselves and to become devoted to that will take you far in your practice.

We have discussed the asanas, our physical postures, movement, and flow. Ashtanga or Raja yoga holds the asanas and our pranayama, our breath work, as two of its principles. Pratyahara is the fifth principle. To review, pratyahara is when you withdraw your senses, controlling the senses both internally and externally. Many yoga postures and asanas mimic this with the physical actions of the body which will help you focus on this principle. What is important is to gain your own independence from your senses.

Some decide to meditate first which is why many yoga classes begin with a brief meditation. As you close your eyes and still your body you can begin paying attention to your external environment, withdraw your senses from what you know, and then focus internally, independent of yourself. Some people tend to focus on their heartbeat to gain internal insight.

The sixth principle is Dharana, which also means concentration. In the perspective of Raja/Ashtanga yoga, you concentrate on your inner thoughts and feelings. To do this, some focus on a physical object like a candle or a space on the wall to help you to delve into concentrating on what you truly and purely think and feel. Distractions are let go of and your mental state can be controlled. Once capturing Dharana, you can begin to meditate, or Dhyana. You begin to hush the thoughts that are coming to your mind through your emotions. Your intelligent self begins to cultivate imagination and become one with the universe. The ego is let go of and you exist in your purest form.

The last and eighth principle is Samadhi, which is translated to mean complete realization where all knowledge comes together as one. The unification of this realization creates the connection with the divine universe. The duality of the self is released, and you can see yourself as one being. We all have good and evil inside us, for example. The categories go away, and you see yourself as what you are. Having all of these principles in mind, you begin the movements of this type of yoga: Raja, also known as Ashtanga.

Bikram Yoga: Some Like It Hot!

Shockingly to some, Bikram Yoga takes place in a heated room reaching 105 degrees! But why? Why would someone want to be in a room that hot without coming out with a tan? There are typically mirrors in the room so you can see your body's radiance as you shift through all of those hot yoga poses, but it might be a weird sensation to be in a hot room and not see the benefits beautifully on your skin, if being tan is your thing.

Well, the benefits of easier stretching, lessened stress, increased flexibility, increased strength, a grander cardiovascular capacity, and muscular workouts are worth leaving the fogged room without bronzing the skin. Plus, the impact the heat and sweat have on your skin is rejuvenating in itself because of the improvement in circulation and your increased inhalation of oxygen. All of this is great for your blood cells.

First, let's make clear that Bikram yoga and Hot yoga are similar, but not exactly the same practice. Bikram is done in a heated room of 105 degrees and 40 percent humidity consisting of 26 yoga poses and breathing exercises. The class is generally 90 minutes long. Alternatively, hot yoga is in a room that is heated above normal standards, usually 80 - 100 degrees with a various number of poses. Hot yoga might include music and human interaction while Bikram is a more silent and independent practice. Both practices have many health benefits for the body and mind.

It is obvious that the heated room will stretch and warm your muscles. You will find, if you compare Bikram or Hot yoga to your other practices, that the poses will become easier to perform and shift through. Your range of motion will astound you. Also, it has been researched that in hot yoga you burn more calories. Trust that you will be able to tell the difference with how much you sweat! Although Bikram might be more intense, Hot yoga will produce the same effects. The benefits will heal your body. Your bones will become stronger, your stress levels will decrease, if you steer towards depression sometimes, performing one of these types of yoga can help with that. Your metabolism will be more efficient as your heart, lungs, and muscles will be working at an optimal pace.

Before you decide to try this practice, try a regular yoga class first. Once deciding to take the leap, make sure that you are hydrated before the class and have a large water bottle on hand. Many prefer to have one with ice so that you can stay hydrated, and make sure that there is water for you when you are disembarking. If you have a pre-existing health condition, ask your doctor if a hot yoga class is good for your health. We don't want you passing out in there, seriously. If you begin to feel dizzy or disoriented, stop and leave the room. It is okay to do so, and you must if you begin feeling those sensations. Wear lightweight and comfortable clothing, bring your own towel and your own yoga mat for hygiene purposes, and consider bringing gloves and socks that have gripping fabric, so you are not slipping and sliding on the mat.

Bikram or Hot yoga is a class that you might have to get used to. Sometimes the first class feels revolutionary and sometimes it is a little too much. People do get used to it, but it is not for everyone and that is okay.

Vinyasa, Power, and Flow Yoga

The flow of yoga is key to going through the motions of shifting poses. This is what Vinyasa yoga is all about. With consistent breath, the harmonious moving from pose to pose is what makes an individual powerful in Power yoga. These terms Vinyasa, Power, and Flow yoga are all interchangeable although some teachers might relate slight differentiations; that is why all of these types of classes have so much variety.

The yoga postures and movements from pose to pose are divergent every class. It is so beneficial for your body to go through inconsistent ranges of motion. That is how you balance your workout so that all parts of your body are exercised. When you are running you have one typical range of motion whereas in yoga you are stretching and giving strength to all parts of the body. The timing of postures change, the sequential order changes, and therefore your body is less succumbed to injury. Philosophically, Vinyasa is an older, sacred form of yoga. Its intention is to relate the yoga session to your life with the realization that you are constantly moving forward. Similarly, your transitions from pose to pose is how you move forward throughout the class.

Vinyasa is appropriately translated to mean "variation," and that is because of the variations of classes and how they structure the pose sequences. As we separate the word's parts, vi is translated to mean "in a special way" and nyasa means "to place." Setting an intention for every movement is how to make sure that you are placing your body in an extra special way. As your body moves, so does your consciousness just as life moves in a variety of ways and how you have to shift your consciousness thusly. It is like we are using our body language to express how we feel just like we do in our daily lives. In class, you will see that just like in life, the postures transition and yet are still connected. You will inhale and exhale through your nose as you go from posture to posture in synchronization. This breath work is known as ujjayi breath. Ujjayi translates to victory just as you will feel victorious moving from pose to pose. You will feel a natural heat that soars through your body, aiding in cardiovascular health. The relaxing yet energetic effects this breath work has on your body will make you a winner because as you breathe, you live!

Depending on the class, Vinyasa yoga can be the height of high performance or a slow and steady moving flow. Regardless, your flexibility will strengthen and be sustained as you continue the discipline. You move through both asanas and standing postures as you breathe consistently through your nostrils. Many teachers will ask you to set an intention for every class at the very beginning so that you can come back to it as the class rises in difficulty and when you are slow moving and meditated. Stick to the present moment; the moves will keep you doing so. When you get distracted by thought, try to return back to your intention and focus on the movements you are cycling through. Become absorbed into the class. Your teacher plans activities for you so you can let go of control on the movements of your physical body. Vinyasa is a meditation where you lose your sense of self to find balance and harmony between each of your movements instead of racing thoughts.

We go from child's pose to savasana, which some call the death pose, just as we do in life. We control what we know, which is our bodily movements and our breath: one of the only aspects that is consistent in life. We learn about ourselves as we use our prana in transitions. Enjoy Sun Salutations and Tadasana instead of focusing on whatever is inside your head. Enjoy the sweat and health benefits as you breathe in and out in rhythm with your stabilized and flowing movement. Also, remember that you are not competing with your classmates. Everyone comes into class at their own level and on their own journey. Hold a pose as long as you can, but steer away from too much pain; if you feel you might get injured or that you are in too much pain, just stop. This is a fun practice so remember: just have fun!

Finally Unlocking the Mystery

And there you have it. On your keychain you have the key to breath work, the key to meditation, and the key to yoga. Having learned the ancient history and modernization of each door, you have a full, well rounded knowledge base that explains why these mindful activities are essential for helping you become more self-aware as to how your mind works and how you can practice controlling your consciousness.

You have learned ways to let go of thoughts and emotions so that they do not control you. You have learned ways to access the divine, become one with yourself, connect with the universe around you, use your life force, understand your body in a spiritual way, and create mantras to keep you disciplined. Oh, but there is so much more to learn once you have started your mindfulness journey.

We now move on to our next chapter where we will learn how to focus on what is important to us. Now that we are more self-aware in our minds, we can steer them in a direction that best serves us in our daily lives. We can begin to focus and be rid of distractions that deter us from our goals.

Chapter 2: Focus: Get Rid of Hocus Pocus

"I don't care how much power, brilliance or energy you have, if you don't harness it and focus it on a specific target, and hold it there you're never going to accomplish as much as your ability warrants."
— Zig Ziglar

Hocus Pocus is not just a cute movie about witches! What we mean by this fun, witchy phrase is that in our lives, we are cursed by the witches of our environments and our minds to become vaguely distracted. Once habitual and random distractions enter our lives, we move farther away from our short-term goals, our long-term goals, and our dreams. Sometimes we sit down and have the greatest intentions to stick to our guns and strive toward what we want, but oftentimes our attention diverts to something that is self-sabotaging. Anything that pulls our focus towards negativity or towards avoidance is a witch that we must hex away. Here we will discuss magical spells that will lead to adjusted focus so that we can get to where we want to be in our lives.

Get in the Zone

One of our overarching goals is to focus and become more productive toward our wants and needs. You are beginning to build habits in your life that will help you get there. Make sure that you use your magic to avoid distractions.

Build a man or woman cave or create an office. Create a space that is committed to your goal so any distraction that can come your way can be avoided. This is the space where you are going to be at precise work. Resist temptations at all costs. Let the people who might become distractions know that you are going to be in the zone and give them times that they can contact you. Use headphones that block off the noises around the house. There is no excuse for multitasking during this time. Use mindfulness to focus your mind if you become distracted.

Create a mantra that will keep you focused. Perhaps do yoga before a time where you need sharp focus. Set an intention for yourself so that you can stick to your calendar and stay in the zone. We will deal with distractions in more detail in a little bit because first, we need to figure out what we want. Once we discover what we want, we can find ways to get what we want while anticipating what distractions to avoid and cope with.

Creating Objectives

An objective is an actionable version of what you want. How can you stay focused when you do not have a clear sense of what you need to do? Once you have your objective painted in your mind, you can decide what tasks need to be done by creating small goals. We will look into creating goals in the next chapter.

The difference between a goal and an objective is that a goal becomes the outcome of action, while the objective is focused on the individual's personal achievement. The objective is focused more internally, and the goal is focused more externally. In order to maintain hyper focus and put emotion behind what you want, your objective can make all the difference because what you want is satisfied internally. Therefore, an objective gives you inspiration to stay focused.

We choose our objectives, they are a personal choice! You have the power, you superhero, you! Now that you have declared yourself a superhero, think about what superheroes need to do to maintain their greatness and prowess. They have to train and practice through experience. We strive for maximal achievement, to get want we want done to the best of our ability, and in order to get that we have to have a positive attitude. Positivity will give way to strong motivation and focus. A positive attitude makes life easier in many ways. Emotions might arise that spawn negativity. We have gained so many coping skills to battle negative emotions through analysis of our thought patterns. We don't want emotions that don't serve us to deter action towards what we want. Make sure to smile a lot! A smile can literally make you happier, so smile even though you might want to scream at the top of your lungs.

When you create objectives for the day, you have set your focus. Whether you decide to write it down or picture yourself reaching the goal in your mind, you need to find a way to meaningfully set an intention. This here is an opportunity for self-discovery. You get to reach deep inside your emotions and your mind to figure out what you want in life. Only then can you incorporate a to-do list so that you can reach that goal or goals.

You cannot skip this first step. To start, write three things that you want so that you can picture that in your mind for the day. Create a list of things that you want that you believe are attainable and things that you want that seem out of reach. Sometimes we set limitations for ourselves that are false. We create all or nothing thought patterns and believe that because you did not achieve what you want in a certain way, it won't work again when using the same tactic. For example, if you decide to send out your resume to jobs or careers that you want and you get rejected, you might generalize and believe that the resume you created will never get you a job that you want. This thought pattern is not necessarily true.

This takes us to our next step: **taking action.** The first topic we can unbox is, do we have the skills to get what we want? If not, you need to find out how to seek the knowledge and wisdom that is required for your particular objective. It is okay not to know everything. In fact, no one does! Be humble; it is okay even if you have to start from scratch.

When we wake up and think about what we want to get done in order to get what we truly want, our motivation can be high or low. If you do not feel like the go getter that you can be, try to refresh and restart your day. Tell yourself positive affirmations. Tell yourself that you are going to have a good day because as long as you do steps one, two, and three, you will feel good about yourself after having met your objective. When you can visualize what you want and what you have to do to get what you want, you will find that focus comes easier than you might believe. Of course, it is very difficult to keep focused for a lengthy amount of time. It is almost impossible to completely avoid distractions.

Dealing with Distractions

Picture this: you have written down a couple of ideas about what you want. You have brainstormed and set an intention or multiple intentions. Once you realize what you have to do for the day, you need to anticipate distractions, or they will get you almost every time. They are sneaky little buggers, too!

Think about part of your to-do list that will create an environment where distractions can leak in. Try to let no distractions cross your path during the times that you are supposed to be in the zone. Once you think deeply about the kind of distractions that can deter you, think about how you can refocus yourself. Now we are going to explore some common distractions and how to deal with their meddling ways!

The Terror of Technology

Ponder upon the duality of technology, for it has a dark side and a light side, similar to that of humanity. It is a little scary how much technology is trying to be more human. You don't have to watch the Terminator to know that technology can be used as a weapon! Technology's weapon is that of distraction when the mood strikes! Our technological assistants (Google, Amazon, Siri, etc.) have become helpful friends and employees instead of merely robots. Our computers, phones, and tablets are our entertainers and our game partners.

There is no judgement though. If you are a professional gamer, then technology works in your favor. The same goes for if you are an influencer. The problem arises when technology becomes a distraction during the time you are supposed to be in the zone.

For most of our objectives we likely need some form of technology such as our computers or our phones. How else are we going to get 500 plus followers on LinkedIn? There are significant phone calls that we have to take and emails we have to respond to. The list goes on and on. Some technology aligns with your objectives in one way or another, but there are other times when technology, amongst other distractions, can lead to less productivity. The less productivity, the lesser chance of gaining satisfaction and fulfillment through what you want. With anticipating your movements towards fighting distractions, you can create behavioral patterns so that the distraction will have less of an effect in the future. You will have created a positive habit! Analysis can also help. Think about your thought patterns. What leads you to the distraction; what triggers it? Does an emotion trigger it? If you understand why the distraction is happening, you can better absolve it.

Oftentimes our tasks include using a computer; your environment might be full of ready distractions. Some use a website blocker or a home page with a message based on focus so you will have a constant reminder to stay in the game. Unless you need your phone, put it on silent. Create a setting that is distraction free. Let your family, friends, and even colleagues know that you are going to be working on something and you cannot be disturbed. This can be in your professional and your personal life.

The Mind's Vacation

Sometimes, our minds like to take a little trip away from our commitments. Once our minds begin to travel and wander about, our focus becomes blurred. It might seem like it is happening out of nowhere, but that is not the case. There is a thought that enters the mind that shifts your focus and diverts your attention elsewhere. That is alright because this is easy to handle.

All it takes is shifting your mind back to your focus and your objective. Use mindfulness in order to resort back to the reality that you desire. Recall your objective and the reasoning behind it. Dig into your emotions and repaint the picture so that your mind can regain its focus. Accept the fact that your mind took a trip and remind yourself of why you need to come back to the task at hand. You always can come back to what you want because it is connected with emotional passion.

Passion can take you farther than you believe to be possible. It will shock your mindset into focusing if you use it to your advantage. Sometimes your mind wants to ignore your passion. It tricks you into procrastination and limits you. If you train your mind to have a sense of urgency about getting what you want, it will be driven to get objectives reached a little more quickly instead of falling prey to distracted thoughts and actions.

Get Your Zzzzz's

Oftentimes when setting objectives, we want to get everything done all at once and that is just impossible. Do not overwhelm yourself. Make sure that your objectives are attainable within that day or that week. Sometimes we want to do too much during the day and there are only 24 hours to do it. Do not forget that you must sleep as well.

Lack of sleep is a form of hocus pocus in itself. Lack of sleep makes your mind dull, less sharpened. It leads to poor decision making. It also makes you tired (obviously), and no one wants to go through their day feeling sleepy and run down. Some even track their sleep so that they can find more motivation during the day. There are so many benefits to getting the right amount of sleep. It is a spell against Hocus Pocus! Make a commitment to setting a bedtime. Create for yourself a nighttime ritual that has a deadline. Set out your clothes for the next day, meditate, take a relaxing shower, and if you want you can even make your coffee for the next day. All of these tasks can set you up for success when you wake up and will put you at ease before you go to sleep.

Meditating and listening to calming music (with or without lyrics) can help you fall asleep instead of reaching for your phone and scrolling through your feed or watching videos. Staring at light from electronics can make falling asleep more difficult. Also, if you do physical activity and exercise during your day, you tend to sleep better. Getting 7-8 hours of sleep is usually recommended, but you might find that a certain number of hours works better for you. Sometimes 6 is the magic number. It all depends on your lifestyle and the length of the stages of sleep that you go through. Some sleep more deeply and some stir at any sound. The goal is to get the most restful sleep possible so that you can wake up motivated and ready to take the day by storm!

Freedom!!!

What actions do you need to take to make your objective a reality while giving yourself space to be free? Setting reminders around your environment can be helpful.

Let's say that you decide that in the afternoon you give yourself an hour lunch and time to watch some television and/or stream videos on social media. Giving yourself freedom is an absolute necessity. It is an impossible expectation to stay focused for the entirety of your waking hours, even for a superhero. Spiderman worked for the newspaper and hung out with Mary Jane; he was not Spiderman 24/7. You need to provide yourself with some down time so that when you are taking action, you can do so with all of your might.

Think about the activities that you enjoy. When you schedule your breaks, try to fill them with enjoyable moments and find gratitude in the work that you have done thus far. Some decide to take a walk in nature during work or eat their lunch outside. Exercising in any way is a delightful way to spend your scheduled freedom. Maybe you want to take time to read something for pleasure instead of something that is task or work related. You might want to sing or dance. Maybe you want to spend your time talking to a loved one, friends and family. Whatever you want to do, do it! Just make sure that you schedule the time because otherwise, distractions can become a free for all; we don't want that!

The Vanishing of Hocus Pocus

We now have tools to take Hocus Pocus out with the trash and find the focus we need to succeed. There can seem to be enemies of distractions coming at you from all sides, but now we know that it can be avoided.

You are able to put your mind through training camp so that it can focus best for you. As you continue to practice recognizing your thought patterns that lead to distractions, you will be able to take on new opportunities that are more challenging and require more time to focus; you will be equipped to focus for a longer period of time. You will see that with focus, your memory will improve. You will notice the benefits of your focus training and continue on the path toward successful objectives. Internally, you will feel the fueling flame of focus within you grow higher and higher. Stress will decrease because you will be more productive. Emotions of guilt from distractions will transform into acceptance and willingness to change. Once you are able to maintain focus and realize your objectives, you can cohesively and knowledgeably create winning goals for yourself.

Chapter 3: The Goal Getter in You

"You can only become truly accomplished at something you love. Don't make money your goal. Instead, pursue the things you love doing, and then do them so well that people can't take their eyes off you."
— Maya Angelou

As our brain sifts through viable information that will lead to a goal, we consider what we want and seek education. We need to figure out what is necessary in order for this goal to be completed. Do we have all of the right tools? Do we know everything we need to know in order to get this done? What kind of preparation is needed before you even start working towards your goal? All of these questions can help guide you towards an achievable goal within your reality.

Once you create an intention for your objectives you will limit distractions. Set these objectives in the morning and write it down. Then, write down a to-do list for the day. Set aside time for productivity and set aside time for when you allow yourself some free time. Saying that you won't succumb to any distraction is not attainable, so setting aside moments where you can live in distraction is healthy just as long as you make sure that your time specific goals can be maintained by the end of the day.

As stated earlier, an objective is an actionable version of what you want. What actions do you need to take to make your objective a reality while giving yourself space to be free?

Setting reminders around your environment can be helpful. Let's say you decide that in the afternoon you give yourself an hour lunch and to watch some television and/or stream videos on social media. Place a reminder so that you know to get back to being productive once the hour is over. You can place a post-it note in an unobtrusive spot (you don't want to ruin your free time with a constant reminder), or set an alarm that is not annoying and demotivating by selecting motivational music instead of the usual siren!

You're Smart! Create a S.M.A.R.T. Goal

Before you decide to focus on your goals, it is best to make one. Often, we do not reach our goals because they are too general and lack focus themselves. First and foremost, make a S.M.A.R.T. goal, a commonly used acronym.

Instead of generalizing, be specific. When we generalize our focus is usually all over the place. It is as if we do not know where to begin. Create a SPECIFIC goal. It should be extremely clear to you what exactly the goal is. It needs to be significant to you, something that drives you and your emotions. When you are emotionally backed you are more driven to reach your goal. Make it simple and specific.

Make sure you can MEASURE your goal. How do you know that you have achieved your goal? Your measurement should be motivating.

Then, make sure that you can <u>ATTAIN</u> your goal. That is why typically creating short term goals and a long-term goal is helpful. Of course, reach for the stars, but if your goal is not analyzed and attainable, it will never happen. We can create goals that we cannot achieve and that are self-sabotaging before we even start. You want to be sure that you are focusing on something you can actually have in your life.

Moreover, your goal should be <u>RELEVANT.</u> It needs to matter most to you, and it needs to align with what you are trying to achieve so that it is worth the effort placed upon it.

Lastly, it needs to be <u>TIME</u> based. Set a time the goal should be completed by. When you create a deadline, you are more likely to structure your focus in a timely manner instead of dilly dallying. Making up a SMART goal for yourself will definitely keep your focus because it will tell you specifically what to do, it will motivate you, you know you can get there, it will matter to you, and you know when it will happen. Having this specificity, this plan, will help keep you focused. Make a calendar so that, regardless of distraction, you will know what you need to accomplish daily so that your timeline sticks.

When creating your goals, remember that they have to be measurable - so try to use a short time frame. This is why making your goals smaller can be helpful. You will feel accomplished by meeting them by your chosen deadline. Sometimes a little pressure can be positive! You will attain what you want, your objective, actionably.

Sticking to It

When writing your goals, you should use an action verb for each one. The whole point is to take action, right? What is so intriguing and personalized is that action verbs are quite dynamic because they can reflect a mentally driven action, emotionally driven action or a physically driven action. The opportunities are endless, and it all promotes you reaching your short goals so that you can reach your super, long term goal. What action verbs do is they describe how to reach an objective. The action verb expresses exactly what you have to do.

For example, if your super goal was to lose 10lbs in a month and one of your daily goals is to meal prep for the weekend, you can make a statement like: "I am going to cook my dinner." The action verb here is cook. This is going to be physically actionable, but it can have a mental and emotional component. It is best when you can have all three to drive you towards your goal. Whenever you seek to do anything, pairing a motivating emotion to it will inspire you to achieve whatever you want to get done. With emotional backing and mental preparation, you will be unstoppable, especially with a shorter deadline. Think about the objective work you can cover when you give yourself shorter deadlines. Just make sure that the shorter deadlines do not lead to stress. Instead, focus on staying focused; this way, you will hold yourself accountable and to a high standard.

Once you've created a goal and a timeline while making a plan for what could possibly distract you, how can you make sure that you will stick to your goals? It is an aspect that needs to be analyzed because creating goals is only the beginning! Now, it is time to take action.

One way to make your goals stick is to stick a picture of you achieving the goal in your mind. If you want to run a half marathon, picture yourself crossing the finish line. Some believe if you visualize things and put them into the universe, in some way, they will come to you. That does not mean that if you have a goal to win the lottery and say it over and over and over, you will win the lotto. You might win a different type of lottery by winning and achieving something luckily or by chance! Try to use strategy to motivate you into achieving your goal. Saying things aloud or in your mind is an affirmation to continue your effort.

Another way that you can keep moving towards your goal is to have someone hold you accountable. Tell a close friend or family member what you are trying to do and what often deters you. They can help you stay focused on your cause! Try to think of your thought patterns and emotional patterns. Maybe you tend to eat unhealthily with your partner. Instead of having them push food on you, let them know what you are trying to do. They can support you instead of helping to sabotage you! Even better, you can surround yourself with those trying to reach the same goal that you are. If you are wanting to finish a half marathon, maybe join a running group.

Furthermore, you should give yourself positive reinforcements, or rewards, for even the smallest of accomplishments towards your goals. You do not have to provide yourself with a humongous gift every time, but if you kindly reward yourself, that will promote further action in that direction. As you go from small goal to small goal, you will start to see changes internally and externally in yourself and in your life. You will begin to believe in yourself and battle the limits you create in your mind. Just keep reminding yourself that you can do anything. Embrace the possibilities and you will find the go getter in yourself!

Chapter 4: Self Control For the Soul

"The first and best victory is to conquer self. To be conquered by self is, of all things, the most shameful and objectionable."
-Plato

There definitely is something to this self-control thing, but for some reason it has a negative connotation. Have you ever heard someone say to you, "Control yourself!" Well, when you are out of control that is definitely the last thing that you want to hear!

Control is powerful and it has a direct effect on the way we behave. There are so many moments in life where we wish we could have controlled ourselves more effectively. Whether you want to control your anger, your eating, your impulses or anything else, you must look more into yourself: who you are. Now, the "self" is a concept, a construct, that needs to be further understood in order for you to properly control it. We speak the words "I" and "me" consistently, but have you ever thought about what those words really symbolize? The Buddha has actually denied that we have a self or a soul, which he called "anatman." Understanding this crucial belief will help you control what you have previously called yourself, but really is something else entirely. To first find control, we need to conquer the idea of the self.

This information should not be mind-shattering and instead should be mind-opening. Don't worry, we still do exist. Everything that you know and love actually does exist, but just does not connect with what we instinctively know as our self. Think on this: how would you define the self? Once you have an idea in your mind, consider the fact that it is what separates you from everyone else in the world. There is a sense of originality about it. There is a connection to your past, present, and future. What of our memories? We were a self in our past? The answer is no. Those are concepts that need to be forgotten. Think of your experience in the present. Realize that your personality traits, your actions, and your body are in fact, not actually connected to one construct. They are separate and they are beautiful. To consider them as one leads to suffering because those attributes as one are quite impossible to control. This idea is also why it is so pertinent to stay in your present, the here and now. We cannot control the past or the future anyway!

How We Talk about Ourselves

Change your vocabulary from "being" to "having." We have and live experiences instead of becoming them. To consider that we are something is to psychologically believe that there are permanent aspects to life. Luckily, we are constantly evolving and as we do so, we try to gain control over our bodies and our behaviors. Our behaviors do not make us who we are, but our behavioral patterns are something that we have or have not. This way, we connect with others who are behaving with us and experiencing life with us. We connect less with ourselves and more with others and the universe.

We are not the centers of the universe; the sun does not revolve around us. Instead, we focus less on what we believe psychologically to be our "self" and it becomes easier to control our experience and separate parts. Our point of view will ultimately shift drastically as we disregard the central idea that we contain a self inside of us in our consciousness. The answer to understanding and releasing what we formerly would have called our "self" is spiritual in nature. Enhanced spirituality is a pathway towards controlling your ever-changing thoughts and behaviors. The one commonality in the individual human experience is personal psychological continuity and that knowledge helps us acquire control over our life experience as it connects with our consciousness and others.

How We Think about Ourselves

Now we focus on introspection and how our thoughts work in separation from what we have identified as ourselves without distraction. We shut away our thoughts of the past and focus on the present experience that is unfolding. We pay attention to our thoughts and make sure that they are not causing any suffering. We do not anticipate or fear the future. We do not narrate to ourselves the mistakes of our past. Instead, we practice mindfulness so that we can remain still in our thoughts and delegate them accordingly. We need to choose optimism over pessimism and become glass half-full people. We need to find gratitude in our experience. Controlling our thoughts can help relieve those that cause us suffering in the present moment. We detach from the idea of the self by embracing reality as it is, as it is happening. We become a selfless observer of our various thoughts and mental states.

The soul is a concept that came about in ancient histories used by philosophers like Plato and Aristotle while also being an affluent topic in many religions. It is a part of us and involved in our emotions, our virtues, morals, perspective, our thoughts, and in part, makes us unique and distinguishes the individual from anyone else. Because it is mystical it is also a theory, but one that we are going to run with for now. Moreover, the soul is considered to be part of our functioning both psychologically and mentally.

Technically speaking, controlling the soul is controlling many parts of your life. Many believe that the soul is what leaves the body when they pass away; it is a mentionable part of our survival; it is a necessity because once it leaves, so does our time in this plane of existence. Philosophically, the soul is not a doer of actions and it does not act on behalf of the individual either. The soul is affected by our behavior but does not commit the process of them. The soul is thought to hold the duality of emotion in us, the light and the dark. The light of love, the dark of hatred, the light of joy and the dark depths of grief. It can give us the courage and the endurance that we need to find control within ourselves and to take action or inaction towards a more fulfilling lifestyle. It takes bravery to look introspectively and decide where we want to learn to gain control. Our soul will thank us for our efforts in doing so as it uses our morality to guide the way. The soul symbolizes human nature and sometimes our nature or nurture needs to be tweaked a bit.

Different Belief Systems

You might not believe in a soul and that is perfectly okay. Many don't! Still, the tactics can be used to control a part of your being. Some might call it your intuition. Instead, many who don't believe in the soul tend to focus on what is tangible: our brains, our bodies, our five senses (some do not believe in the sixth sense), and the physical environment around us. The subject of consciousness is a metaphysical and existential one that might never be answered in our lifetimes. A personality is that of nature and nurturing. We have free will. That is all you need for control - the knowledge that you can use your free will to control your actions and thought patterns. Both those who believe and those who don't believe will be able to use their brain and create positive functioning. We guide our intelligence and our emotions so that we can be satisfied with our new and shiny lifestyle habits.

Whether you believe in the concept of a soul or not, there are still tactics to maintaining control of your impulses, your behaviors, and your thoughts. We will dig into controlling your emotions in a later chapter! As we take away the guise of the self, we can look upon these psychological benefactors each with a different lens. We use our brain power to master the goal of control. We make impactful and tactical decisions with our mind, the control tower. We must admit that control is not permanent; it is a practice. It is normal for the finding of control to go in waves. Sometimes we are riding the waves and sometimes we might falter, but that does not mean we can't get back on the boogie board! Recall that we have the experience of control instead of becoming controlling. If we fall off, that does not mean that we have utterly fallen. That is why removing the self from these practices is beneficial in perspective.

Observe where in your life you feel that you need control of what is immaterial and intangible so that you can create a plan to maneuver with. Think about the parts of your life where you find you need more control. Common goals for control are controlling your eating, your impulses, use of substances, your finances, and negative thought patterns. Of course, with each unique individual there are parts of a personal life that might need some control, but this list is generalized to match common issues.

An Example: Food Control

If you want to control the food you eat so that you can lose weight and have a healthier body, make a plan to avoid temptation and one that you can consistently stick to. Control is not considered to be a punishment and it is definitely not self-deprivation. Depriving yourself is something that usually does not last long term. The goal here is to try to formally change your behavior patterns in a meaningful way.

When you go to the grocery store, avoid the sections that you believe you should. If you want to control your sugar intake, stay away from that bakery! Make a meal prepping plan and bring your healthy food and snacks with you wherever you go. Create an exercise routine so that you can burn the food that you intake properly. Let others know about your goals so they can hold you accountable for what you are trying to control. There are many apps that are available to help you. There are calorie counters, food logs, exercise logs, articles and books that you can read. These resources give you habitual patterns that can help you gain control until you can do it on your own.

If you are gearing towards controlling your impulses, you are going to have to slow down! We often believe that we are making impulsive decisions. Sometimes it is a repeated behavioral pattern, but more often than not, it is because we do not slow down and think before we act. We have discussed being mindful, which is the answer to controlling impulsivity. Our world is on go mode all of the time. We live in a very fast and evolving world and that tends to make us go at a faster pace.

The key here is that we don't have to, and we should not. We need to go at our own pace because we are on our own journey. Everyone has their own path. Before acting, stop and think. What is the thought pattern that is moving the body towards acting? Perhaps you are working with a colleague that gets under your skin. Are you quick to lash out? Instead, take a deep breath and think before you speak. Breath work is the trick up your sleeve to avoid impulsivity. Further, there are ways to circumnavigate your impulsivity. Write what you would have said to your peer in your journal instead of at them. Question yourself. Are you really going to say what you want to say? Do you need to say it? Is it you that should say it at this very moment? It is always positive to stop and question yourself. It is that introspection that can help you find better control.

Finances are always a reliable topic because everyone wants control over their money. Some are worry free, but a vast majority wish they had more control over their finances; it is undeniable. It could be overspending while shopping at the mall or something more serious that puts you into debt that you cannot afford. The advice is usually to budget, but that is not as easy as the word states! It takes conscious decision making and planning on our part to commit to a budget. It takes decreasing some of our known behaviors that lead to spending too much money. Whether you have to commit to meal planning instead of buying from restaurants or finding a budgeting app to help you out, controlling your finances can be done.

Take out your journal and take a hard look at your expenses against how much income you are earning. Try to put what you can into savings, but while being realistic about your budget. Plan ahead for your spending and stick to it. Possibly have someone from your family hold you accountable and help guide you. Find the financial advisor of the family, or heck, if you can afford it, maybe seek out a financial advisor. Once you find the behaviors that lead towards you overspending you find ways to overcome them. If it happens to be shopping too much at the mall, stay away from the mall! It is doable and you can do it.

An Example: Substance Control

Substance abuse has become a worldwide epidemic. If you are taking more medication than you know you should or if you have unfortunately suffered from addiction, there are many avenues to travel toward so that you can find recovery to control your use. Alcoholics Anonymous and Narcotics Anonymous can help give you the support and literal steps you need towards being able to control this self-sabotaging habit so that you can build a better lifestyle for yourself. They teach you how to forgive and accept yourself. They help you build relationships with your loved ones if your using substances has forsaken them. They help you deal with the emotional ramification of your suffering. Many seek therapy as well. Just know that you are not alone whatsoever. There are so many people who have an issue controlling the substances they use. The right groups and contacts will teach you how to cope with negative thinking and adverse behavior using many of the coping skills already outlined here, plus a little more in depth for that topic area. You take an inventory of yourself: your assets, defects, the relationships that you have, your behavioral patterns and how they affect you and how you can mend them.

Shutting Down the Negativity

Controlling negative thinking in general is something that can be reversed into positive thinking, but again, it takes practice. This practice will help you avoid the feeling that you are spiraling out of control. Plus, it is a cool trick to be able to control your mind!

First, write down all of the negative thoughts that you can recall entering your mind. You can categorize these thoughts by subject or any other categorical figuring that suits you. Next, write down a counter thought, a motivating thought. Here is where the practice comes in. When those thoughts tend to trigger your mind, you need to immediately think the positive thought that you created for yourself. After practicing this consistently these counter thoughts will become automatic. Your thought patterns will become clearer to you as you write them down. Finding the root of the thought can help you come up with a purposeful counter thought that will resonate with you and make a difference in your overall attitude.

As you analyze some of these thoughts, try to make sure that they are rooted in reality. Many times, we have thoughts that just are not true. You might tell yourself that you always fail, when that is absolutely, one hundred percent inaccurate. You are a success! Dig a little deeper and figure out what part of your story makes you feel the most successful and stick to that. We must accept that we have negative thoughts, it is only natural. We must also accept that it is our responsibility to take the control away from them by bringing positivity and light to the mind.

Controlling your mind, body, and spirit will work wonders for you. Your mind will blossom, your body will thank you, and your soul (if you believe in such a thing) will emit gratitude to the highest degree. The point is, you are trying to moderate. Your thought patterns reveal themselves and you find ways to talk to your mind instead of battling it. This is all for the greater good. You can gaze at your triggers, thoughts, and behaviors so that you can freshly, with wide, open eyes, decipher how you want to cope with the ones that don't serve you. There is a way to cope with anything, but you need to put in the effort, the consistency, and the commitment to the practice. This is a lifelong practice. We tend towards certain thoughts and behaviors through nurture and nature so just make sure that you are kind as you walk along this part of your journey.

Chapter 5: Make Willpower Your Superpower

"Willpower is the key to success. Successful people strive no matter what they feel by applying their will to overcome apathy, doubt, or fear."
- Dan Millman

The will is a powerful tool, just like our minds. If we want to make something happen, we can use our will to make it happen. Just the thought of that is exciting. The goal is to find the power within us so that we can use our will toward our objectives in accordance with the lifestyle that we want to live. Our will distinguishes us from any other species which makes us so special. We have the power to contemplate our impulses, pause before we act, and analyze our thoughts and feelings. There is an innate nature, but we are evolved and therefore, we can manipulate our own lives. We control what we have the ability to control, and that is always more than you think. You have more power inside you than you know. It is time to become acquainted with the power of your will so you can use it for your best interests in mind.

Part of willpower is inaction - deciding not to do something that you want to do. It is not an easy feat to decide to say "no." Many have an issue with saying the word "no" in general, especially the people pleasers out there! When some think of willpower, it is common for the mind to think about not eating the large chocolate cookie at Starbucks, but it can go deeper than that. You might want to say no to go out drinking with your friends because you have to meet a deadline for work. Humans instinctively want to be instantly gratified, it is only natural. We seek as much pleasure as we can as we run away from pain.

Sometimes using willpower feels painful because we are saying no to something that we might really want. The wonderful thing to know is that you can do it. You can say "no." You have that power and that is a freeing feeling. You need to seek the will inside of you and know that you have the free will to say that word.

We don't like to hear the word "no" when we are children, so it is hard to say no to others, and especially hard when we want to say it to ourselves. We need to speak to our inner child and kindly say "no." We need to understandingly tell our friends that we need to keep our priorities in order and do our work instead of going out. Delaying gratification is okay because it gives us something to look forward to. It might be easier to say to yourself "not right now." Think of why you are saying "no." You are not eating that cookie because you want to be a healthier person. You want to lose weight or keep your sugar levels down. Think of something healthier to do instead like exercise. Reward yourself with self-care. Reward yourself for using your willpower. If you focus on what you want, it will be amazing to see what you are willing to say "no" to. Keep your objective and goals in mind on a daily basis so that moment by moment you will find the willpower within you to speak to yourself so that you can be your own guide towards success.

In order to thrive in your willpower, it is important to make sure that you get enough rest. Our best decision making happens when we are not tired. A tired brain makes for lazy decision making. It takes great effort and strength to use your willpower because it is against what you naturally want to do. It takes mindful thought to analyze what you want so that you can push your will and action towards it. In order for you to have the energy to drive your own thoughts and find that power, you need to consistently recharge.

Consider yourself a battery! You don't need to keep going and going and going. We want to be energizer bunnies, but that is not sustainable in the long term. Batteries do run low, and when they do, they need to be changed or charged. We change moment by moment, so we have to be able to recognize and control with our own power those changes. Those changes symbolize our decision making which allows us to evolve in every moment. Take note of when you are feeling exhausted so that you can make restful moments for yourself so that in your waking times you can use your willpower effectively.

Positive reinforcement can also help you sustain willpower long term, but we want to make sure that these rewards *are* actually positive. For example, if you are using your willpower to work out, you do not want to reward yourself with that chocolate chip cookie. Make sure that the reward is also aligned with what you desire. In contrast, reward yourself with a gym class that you have been wanting to try! The enjoyment that you will glean from a challenging hot yoga class will be rewarding enough to keep your willpower going strong for the next time. You use your memory to recall how you used your willpower and how grand it made you feel.

If you do falter, do not forget to be nice to yourself. The use of willpower will ebb and flow like anything else. The wave we are surfing on might get bumpy at times, but we get up and we try to surf again. Positive self-talk will keep your mood on the up and up. We do not want to add stress to our lives because that will negate the willpower, we are growing without ourselves. We are training for a marathon here. You might miss a couple of days. You might need to rest or take a stretch day. Think of your willpower in that way - we try to get up and go so that daily we are working towards our goal, but it is perfectly natural to be imperfect! Make changes that you can manage. Set small goals for using your willpower so that you can celebrate your successes!

The goal is to try to be your best future self. Keeping this in mind you realize that you are formally investing in yourself. This investment will give you the power to use your free will to the best of your ability. That is the point: to just try your best. As long as you know that you are putting in your greatest effort, there is no telling how far you can go as you find the power to use your will!

Chapter 6: Emotions! Regulate and Celebrate

"It is very important to understand that emotional intelligence is not the opposite of intelligence, it is not the triumph of heart over head – it is the unique intersection of both."
- David Caruso

Controlling our emotions is imperative to being able to reach our full potential. Sometimes our emotions tend to rule us and lead to making poor decisions. It takes internal perception to become self-aware of how our emotions affect us. We already know that we are intelligent beings capable of amazing adventures. Now, we must focus our intelligence on our feelings. We need to look into how our circumstances make us feel. Sometimes environments stir up feelings, others bring us feelings, and we are the cause of how we feel. Once we are able to become aware and recognize what we are feeling we can analyze them and discover why we are feeling them. After we determine the cause of our feelings, we can become mindful about how we act according to how we feel.

When you are feeling some type of way, try to come up with a word to encapsulate the feeling. Emotions are mostly intangible so coming up with a word or phrase to describe them might not be the easiest thing in the world. There are multiple websites with lists of feeling words. When you find a word on the list that matches how you feel, you will be more inclined to comprehend the feeling as a whole. In a way, you are expressing to yourself definitively how you feel. Once you have gained self-awareness, you can try to figure out the cause of the emotion. This should be done with both positive and negative feelings. We have both the light and the dark within us, and it is the same with our emotions. We must understand both the yin and the yang. When you have understood the cause of the emotion you can go backwards and try to identify the trigger of the cause that led to the emotion. Once this process is complete you can add the thoughts that arise from the emotion's situation. Then, you can fully understand why an emotion can control how you behave.

If you can commit to this journey the benefits will take you toward a more satisfying life. You will form better relationships with those around you and with yourself. Regulating your emotions is a magical form of self-care and it makes going through life much easier. Internally and externally, you will have gained control after examining your emotions and how they enter and exit your life moment by moment.

A good place to start is usually the beginning. Once an emotion hits, there is a deep impact that gets registered in the mind and body. This can be a positive or a negative emotion and its effects. Try to ask yourself some simple questions. Did the impact of the emotion add any conflict to your life? Does it put a strain on any of the environments you are settled in? Is the emotion a pure outburst instead of an emotion that can be stabilized?

Honesty is Key
Be honest with yourself. Make sure that your emotions are not causing you to put yourself in any danger. Some emotions are very difficult to cope with. There are circumstances of trauma that cause intense emotions. There are some people who react to emotions through sexual activity or substance abuse. If your reaction to emotions becomes serious, then seeking help is the right idea.

The key is accepting our emotions for what they are and what they do to us. We need acceptance before we can kindly manipulate our emotions into regulation. We are not going to repress our emotions. There is no need to use a defense mechanism. It is good that you are feeling the emotion. The emotion is trying to tell you something and that should not be ignored. We commonly repress or suppress anxiety, depression, fear, doubt, tension, pain, and stress. These emotions are difficult to handle so we want them to just go away. Sitting in them will not help but understanding them will. That is what healthy emotional intelligence is. If we are depressed, we consider why we feel depression, what made us sad or upset. What triggered that emotion? With knowledge, the healing can begin, and regulation will occur.

Once you acknowledge these areas around the emotion, it is time to fact check! Sometimes our emotions overrule us and drive us away from reality. Check out your situation with your new reality goggles on. Make sure that the thoughts centered around the emotion are grounded in reality. It is not that your emotions are not valid, but your mind can warp situations into making you feel a certain emotion. It might pursue irrational fear when there is nothing to be afraid of. You might make an assumption about someone else's thoughts that make you feel a certain way. Our minds can take us to faraway places, and we need to steer them back home so that we can get our emotions in check. So, consider all alternatives. Think out of the box because it might help you with regulating your emotions. Even if you have to talk to yourself - there is nothing to be afraid of.

Tips for Controlling Emotions

Keeping a journal that tracks your moods (there are apps as well nowadays) can help you monitor how you feel. You can express clearly and go back to how you have dealt with your emotions in the past. You can look back upon common repercussions of your emotions and successes of regulation. Noticing patterns always helps fuel learning wisdom! Accepting mood patterns can do wonders for your mentality and behavioral patterns. It allows you to become more comfortable with who you are. Your satisfaction from regulation will soar from the moments of clarity.

Remember your breath work? Deep breathing can help immensely in regulating your emotions. When anger peeks, fear strikes, anxiety shakes, and depression drops you, a compassionate deep breathing exercise can help the intensity descend. Calm breathing gives you a moment to think about how you're feeling with rationality. It gives you another focus if only for a couple of moments. Sometimes you realize you need to separate yourself from the situation for a bit or even completely. It is okay to back away and back off. Walking away is not a sign of defeat, but a sign of regulating. Of course, you do not need to habitually run away from your problems, but sometimes giving some space will help. Even if that means shifting your focus. Think about something comical, talk to someone who will give you positive vibes, or go out for a short walk in nature.

Stress most of all can be one of the most difficult emotions to handle and there are so many causes of it throughout life. There are healthy options to alleviate it. Exercise can be a humongous asset to you during those stressful times. Use mindfulness and meditation practices that we have chatted about before or find activities that you love to do, where you find passion, so that you can take a little vacation from your life's stressors.

Finally, as you continue on the journey of regulating your emotions, don't forget to celebrate yourself. Emotions are controlling and learning to control *them* instead is a sensitive and rewarding experience. When you win a battle, use positive reinforcement. Celebrate yourself! If you find a way to curve stress with a tactic that you can consistently use, do something kind for yourself. If you track your mood for a week and discover a divergent path for yourself that helps regulate your emotions, celebrate! Celebrating life and little successes will mean the world to you and will help you continue on your path towards becoming the best you!

Chapter 7: Happy Healthy Habits!

"Chains of habit are too light to be felt until they are too heavy to be broken."
- Warren Buffet

Finding a balance that provides you with happiness is one of the keys to building a better lifestyle for yourself. Here are some habits that you can easily integrate into your life:

Practice Gratitude

Finding things to be thankful for as much as you can throughout your daily life can do wonders for your perspective. Make a gratitude list every so often or you can do so once a day in the morning or at night. You might see a pattern as you continually write your list. The same things or people might keep popping up and you will find an even deeper gratitude for them.

When you find the gratitude in life, some of the little things that get to us will slip away. If you are dealing with a moment that seems dark, try to find the light. Practicing gratitude will keep you aware of all of the wonderful things that are involved in your life. Remember that there are many things to be grateful for and one of those things is yourself.

Keep Up with Your Zzzzzz's

Make sure to get meaningful rest! It will help with decision making on a daily basis. Sleeping is a form of self-care. We need to make sure to get proper rest. If you are finding that insomnia is creeping in, try to do breath-work or meditate before bedtime. Drink a cup of hot tea or take a warm bath. Make an effort of into getting your sleep regiment regularly. If sleep becomes an issue, there are apps now that track your sleep! If you get a solid amount of rest, you will be more productive, have more energy, have higher concentration functioning, and feel happier all around.

Eat Healthy

Eating healthier can do you an insane amount of good. When you eat healthier your body, mind, and spirit just feel better. Try to be mindful when you are eating so that you can savor all of the nutritious goodness! When you eat more mindfully and a little more slowly the food will actually taste better. The health benefits for eating more healthily are infinite. You will have better cardiovascular health, less risk for diabetes; the list goes on and on. Plus, you will have more energy to do the things that you love to do. Your skin will shine, and your smile will widen. Eating healthier is pleasing and if you do so consistently you will feel the difference that it makes in your life.

Work It Out

Pack in exercise most days out of the week. Just like eating healthier, including exercise in your life will change you for the better in an innumerable number of ways. Your bones and muscles will become stronger, and it will put pep in your step as your endurance builds. You will be able to tackle anything with consistent exercise! Do some of the yoga we spoke about, run outside or take a new gym class. You might find something that you love to do and stick to it or you can put some variety in your gym jam so that you can reach your full potential.

Drop Technology

We live in a very fast and innovative world. Most of our lives consist of using some form of technology at almost every moment. Taking some time to put your phone away, get off the computer, shut the TV off, and wind down with yourself will warm your heart. Get out in nature so that you can connect with the outer world. You will build more intimate relationships this way with others and with yourself. The more that you give yourself time away from technology the more that you have time to connect with yourself.

Chapter 8: Everyday Mindful Moments

"Mindfulness isn't difficult, we just need to remember to do it."
- Sharon Salzberg

We have talked in great detail about mindfulness, so bringing that back to the forefront is imperative! Taking mindful moments throughout your day is what is going to help you with anything and everything. It will help you connect with the power in yourself so that you can enact your will the way that you really want to. Here are some ways that you can insert mindfulness in your daily life!

Plan a Mindful Moment

Set a time for yourself where you know that you will be free. Maybe it is before bedtime, when you wake up in the morning, your lunch break at work or on a commute. Take some time to focus on your breathing and check in with how you're feeling. Close your eyes if it feels comfortable for you. Try to listen to what is around you. Engage your senses as much as you can. This is a perfect way to take time for yourself. You are setting aside time for self-care. Putting yourself on pause so that you can be mindfully present is a wonderful habit to create. It is a positive conscious choice that will make you feel wonderfully good. You can become more aware of your attitude and shift accordingly if you want to. Do a quick body scan if you're in the mood.

Meditate Meditate Meditate...*Ommmm*

Meditation on a daily basis, whether it is for five minutes or for more, is one of the best ways for you to stay mindful. You will be able to reach internally as you get to know yourself more and more. You will find more love for yourself if you do. Perhaps use a visualization technique. You can picture that you are at your most favorite place in the whole world. Really place yourself there. Use all of your senses to help your vision. Maybe you are already in a peaceful place. Try listening intently to where you are. Try to clear your thoughts away and just focus on what it is to beautifully exist.

Set an Intention

When you wake up to start your day, set an intention. Think about the things that you desire. What are your goals and objectives? Knowing the things that you want to accomplish can help you mindfully guide your day from moment to moment. If you deeply understand and contemplate on what you want, you can hold that with you throughout your day to keep you inspired and to keep you motivated.

It feels perfect to end on mindful intention. Making a commitment to invest in yourself is worthy of ultimate attention. An intention will focus you on your goals and make you more mindful about what you want and how that makes you become a better and brighter you. You can use your intention to set mindfulness goals and times where you can relax and be with yourself. You can set a goal to do yoga. You can set an intention to read more about things that you love. You can set an intention for changing a habit or for strengthening your willpower. You have so much power inside of you and it only needs to be tapped into and given mindful attention. There is so much about you that there is to know that is under the surface and there is so much about you that there is to know even on the surface and as long as you are mindful, you will have an internal relationship that grows throughout your lifetime.

When we realize that every moment, even the tiniest ones, are moments, then we can learn to become more mindful of them. Those moments that we might consider little are actually not. They are significant. When we learn to notice them, we will be more mindful when seemingly larger moments arise. We will be able to accept ourselves for where we are because we always take us with us everywhere! That is a wonderful thing because everywhere we go, our best friend is there beside us helping us along the way.

Our daily mindful moments will awaken us to all possibilities in our lives. We will know what we are doing and where we are going. We will see our world for what it is and accept it and who we are with open arms. That is the miracle. That is the key to unlocking the mystery. We gain wisdom and find self-love that becomes a burning flame. We find within ourselves what matters most internally, throughout our environment, and in our relationships with others. You become a beacon of truth.

You are brave.

You are brilliant.

You are worthy.

You are special.

You can be mindful.

You can regulate your emotions.

You can reach your goals.

You are extraordinary.

You are love.

References:

A. (2018, June 18). *5 Steps to Writing Clear and Measurable Learning Objectives*. The Bob Pike Group. https://www.bobpikegroup.com/trainer-blog/5-steps-to-writing-clear-and-measurable-learning-objectives

A Beginner's Guide to the 7 Chakras and Their Meaning. (2016, December 18). A Beginner's Guide to the 7 Chakras and Their Meaning. https://www.healthline.com/health/fitness-exercise/7-chakras

Academy, H. (2021). Publisher's Desk: A Hindu View of Mindfulness - Magazine Web Edition October/November/December 2019 - Publications - Hinduism Today Magazine. Publisher's Desk: A Hindu View of Mindfulness - Magazine Web Edition October/November/December 2019 - Publications - Hinduism Today Magazine. https://www.hinduismtoday.com/modules/smartsection/item.php?itemid=5956

Alfonsi, D. (2021, January 12). *How to Do Transcendental Meditation (Step-by-Step Guide)*. Lifehack. https://www.lifehack.org/848704/how-to-do-transcendental-meditation

Ancient Theories of Soul (Stanford Encyclopedia of Philosophy). (2009, April 22). Stanford Encyclopedia of Philosophy. https://plato.stanford.edu/entries/ancient-soul/

Bhagavad Gita Quotes (Author of Bhagavad Gita). (2021). Bhagavad Gita Quotes (Author of Bhagavad Gita). https://www.goodreads.com/author/quotes/8126474.Bhagavad_Gita

Bhagvad GitaÂs Guide to Mindfulness -Atlanta Dunia. (2015, December 15). Bhagvad GitaÂs Guide to Mindfulness - Atlanta Dunia. http://www.atlantadunia.com/dunia/Features/F242.htm

Bryant, K. (2020, August 11). *Getting to Know the Vrittis •*. Yoga Basics. https://www.yogabasics.com/connect/getting-to-know-the-vrittis/

Burgin, T. (2014, September 19). *The Inward Journey Through the Koshas •*. Yoga Basics. https://www.yogabasics.com/learn/the-inward-journey-through-the-koshas/

Burgin, T. (2020a, January 24). *The Mysterious Kundalini •*. Yoga Basics. https://www.yogabasics.com/learn/the-mysterious-kundalini/

Burgin, T. (2020, June 11). *History of Yoga •*. History of Yoga •. https://www.yogabasics.com/learn/history-of-yoga/

Burgin, T. (2020c, June 11). *Mudras •*. Yoga Basics. https://www.yogabasics.com/learn/mudras/

Burgin, T. (2020b, November 28). *Tantra Yoga – Defined and Demystified* •. Yoga Basics. https://www.yogabasics.com/learn/tantra-yoga-demystified/

Burgin, T. (2020d, November 28). *Understanding the Flow of Prana (Life-Force Energy)* •. Yoga Basics. https://www.yogabasics.com/learn/the-flow-of-prana/

Campbell, C. (2019, March 7). *The Dalai Lama Has Been the Face of Buddhism for 60 Years. China Wants to Change That*. Time. https://time.com/longform/dalai-lama-60-year-exile/#:%7E:text=The%20Dalai%20Lama%20is%20considered,sits%20veiled%20behind%20the%20Himalayas.

Co., T. D. (2020, May 19). *6 Inspiring Zen Buddhist Principles That Will Change Your Life*. The Denizen Co. https://www.thedenizenco.com/journal/zen-buddhist-principles

Cronkleton, E. (2019, April 9). *10 Breathing Techniques*. Healthline. https://www.healthline.com/health/breathing-exercise#resonant-breathing

Dellert, N. (2018, October 23). *What Is a Sound Bath? Discover the Benefits of the Meditative Practice*. Allure. https://www.allure.com/story/sound-bath-meditation-benefits

Edblad, P. (2019, October 21). *48 Tiny Habits That Will Make You Awesome - Better Humans*. Medium. https://betterhumans.pub/48-tiny-habits-that-will-make-you-awesome-d8e3959840c8

Eriksson, K. (2020, March 29). *Qigong 101: How to Get Started - Better Humans*. Medium. https://betterhumans.pub/qigong-101-how-to-get-started-2118c3f4d38d

Estrada, J. (2020, January 24). *How to Use Qigong Meditation to Harness the Healing Energy of Your Body*. Well+Good. https://www.wellandgood.com/qigong-meditation/

Gunaratana, B. H. (2019, May 28). *What Exactly is Vipassana Meditation?* Tricycle: The Buddhist Review. https://tricycle.org/magazine/vipassana-meditation/

Harris, S. (2015). *Waking Up: A Guide to Spirituality Without Religion* (Reprint ed.). Simon & Schuster.

History.com Editors. (2018, August 21). *Transcendentalism*. HISTORY. https://www.history.com/topics/19th-century/transcendentalism

How Emotionally Intelligent Are You? (2020, June 3). Verywell Mind. https://www.verywellmind.com/what-is-emotional-intelligence-2795423

K, L. (2020, March 1). *The 9 Zen Principles That Probably Saved My Life*. Let's Reach Success. https://letsreachsuccess.com/zen-principles

L., & L. (2020, June 12). *7 Chakra Crash Course: A Beginner's Guide To Awakening Your Seven Chakras*. Chakras.Info. https://www.chakras.info/7-chakras/

M. (2021, January 11). *An Easy Beginner's Guide To Chakra Meditation.* Mindvalley Blog. https://blog.mindvalley.com/chakra-meditation/#:%7E:text=So%2C%20when%20you've%20identified,clear%2C%20and%20balance%20your%20chakras.

Meditation That's Music to Your Stressed Mind. (2020). Verywell Mind. https://www.verywellmind.com/how-to-practice-music-meditation-3144791

mindfulness. (1828). The Merriam-Webster.Com Dictionary. https://www.merriam-webster.com/dictionary/mindfulness

Nanda, B. R. (2021, February 12). *Mahatma Gandhi | Biography, Education, Religion, Accomplishments, Death, & Facts.* Encyclopedia Britannica. https://www.britannica.com/biography/Mahatma-Gandh

O'Brien, M. (2019, April 23). *11 Ways to Bring More Mindfulness into Your Life Today.* Mrs. Mindfulness. https://mrsmindfulness.com/11-ways-to-bring-more-mindfulness-into-your-life-today/

Online, I. E. (2018, August 19). *How the Buddha gained enlightenment.* The Indian Express. https://indianexpress.com/article/parenting/learning/buddha-enlightenment-nirvana-5288593/#:%7E:text=He%20sat%20in%20the%20lotus,and%20concentrated%20on%20his%20breathing.&text=Sitting%20cross%2Dlegged%20in%20meditation,so%20after%20the%20Buddha's%20posture.

On Psychoacoustic Studies of Didgeridoo. (2021, March 3). The BMJ. https://www.bmj.com/content/332/7536/266/rr

Palermo, E. (2015, March 10). *What is Qigong?* Livescience.Com. https://www.livescience.com/38192-qigong.html#:%7E:text=Qigong%20(pronounced%20chee%2Dgong),controlled%20breathing%20and%20movement%20exercises.&text=Qigong%20is%20therefore%20sometimes%20translated,qigong%20practiced%20throughout%20the%20world.

Patel, D. (2018, December 12). *7 Proven Strategies for Overcoming Distractions*. Entrepreneur. https://www.entrepreneur.com/article/324560

Raja Yoga. (2021). Raja Yoga. https://www.yogaindailylife.org/system/en/the-four-paths-of-yoga/raja-yoga

Raypole, C. R. (2020, April 28). *How To Become The Boss Of Your Emotions*. Healthline. https://www.healthline.com/health/how-to-control-your-emotions#consider-the-impact

Rivers, C. (2020, December 1). *Top 7 Tips: Beginners Visualization Techniques*. EnVision. https://envision.app/2019/08/21/top-7-beginner-tips-visualization-techniques/

Saal, K. (2020, October 21). *What is Vinyasa Yoga? | Vinyasa Flow Yoga Explained*. One Flow Yoga. https://oneflowyoga.com/blog/what-is-vinyasa-yoga

Scott, S. J. (2020b, November 17). *57 Thich Nhat Hanh Quotes on Mindfulness (To Live a More Meaningful Life)*. Develop Good Habits. https://www.developgoodhabits.com/thich-nhat-hanh-quotes/

Self Control. (2021). Psychology Today. https://www.psychologytoday.com/us/basics/self-control

Sitaramananda, S. (2018, October 28). *Yoga Meditation - What is Yoga Meditation?* Sivananda Yoga Farm. https://sivanandayogafarm.org/what-is-yoga-meditation/

Syman, S., Marglin, A. T. T. E., Deshpande, R., Alpert, Y. M., Tomaine, G., Terry, W., & Patricia Karpas, Meditation Studio. (2007, October 1). *The First Book of Yoga: The Enduring Influence of the Bhagavad Gita*. Yoga Journal. https://www.yogajournal.com/yoga-101/first-book-yoga/

The 14th Dalai Lama. (2017, July 12). *Teaching 'Stages of Meditation' and 'Thirty-seven Practices of....* https://www.dalailama.com/news/2017/teaching-stages-of-meditation-and-thirty-seven-practices-of-bodhisattvas-at-disket

The Editors of Encyclopaedia Britannica. (2021). *Krishna | Story, Meaning, Description, & Legends*. Encyclopedia Britannica. https://www.britannica.com/topic/Krishna-Hindu-deity

The Editors of Encyclopaedia Britannica. (2021b). *qi | Definition & Facts*. Encyclopedia Britannica. https://www.britannica.com/topic/qi-Chinese-philosophy

Vipassana Meditation. (2021). Vipassana Meditation. https://www.dhamma.org/en/about/vipassana

What Are Sound Baths? (2020, June 30). Verywell Mind. https://www.verywellmind.com/what-are-sound-baths-4783501

Why There Is No Self: A Buddhist View for the West. (2018, February 18). Iai news. https://iai.tv/articles/why-there-is-no-self-a-buddhist-perspective-for-the-west-auid-1044

Xiao, Q. (2017). *The Mindful Self: A Mindfulness-Enlightened Self-view.* Frontiers. https://www.frontiersin.org/articles/10.3389/fpsyg.2017.01752/full#:%7E:text=Principally%2C%20mindfulness%20in%20Buddhist%20teaching,no%20self.%E2%80%9D%20According%20to%20Buddhism

Yang, J. (2020, July 3). *10 Lessons from The Willpower Instinct | Kelly McGonigal.* Medium. https://jackyangzzh.medium.com/9-lessons-from-the-willpower-instinct-by-kelly-mcgonigal-869d5d8ece43

Yoga for Everyone. (2021). Yoga For Everyone. https://www.nytimes.com/guides/well/beginner-yoga

www.ingramcontent.com/pod-product-compliance
Lightning Source LLC
Chambersburg PA
CBHW071452070526
44578CB00001B/320